OXFORD

A GENEALOGICAL BIBLIOGRAPHY

— BY —
STUART A. RAYMOND

Published by the
Federation of Family History Societies,
c/o The Benson Room, Birmingham & Midland Institute,
Margaret Street, Birmingham, B3 3BS, U.K.

Copies also available from:
S.A. & M.J. Raymond, 6 Russet Avenue, Exeter, Devon, EX1 3QB, U.K.

Text processed and printed by
Oxuniprint, Oxford University Press

Cataloguing in publication data:

RAYMOND, Stuart A., 1945- .
Oxfordshire: a genealogical bibliography. British genealogical bibliographies.
Birmingham, England: Federation of Family History Societies, 1993.

DDC: 016.9291094257

ISBN: 1 872094 57 0

ISSN: 1033-2065

CONTENTS

INTRODUCTION

This bibliography is intended primarily for genealogists. It is, however, hoped that it will also prove useful to historians, librarians, archivists, research students, and anyone else interested in the history of Oxfordshire. It is intended to be used in conjunction with my *English genealogy: an introductory bibliography*, and the other volumes in the *British genealogical bibliographies* series. A full list of these volumes appears on the back cover.

Many genealogists, when they begin their research, do not realise just how much information has been published, and is readily available in printed form. Not infrequently, they head straight for the archives, rather than checking printed sources first. In so doing, they waste much time, and also impose needless wear and tear on irreplaceable archives. However, when faced with the vast array of tomes possessed by major reference libraries, it is difficult to know where to begin without guidance. This bibliography is intended to point you in the right direction. My aim has been to list everything relating to Oxfordshire that has been published and is likely to be of use to genealogists. In general, I have not included works which are national in scope but which have local content. Many such works may be identified in *English genealogy: an introductory bibliography*, to which reference is made at appropriate points below. I have also excluded the numerous notes and queries found in *O.F.H.* and similar journals, except where the content is of importance. Where I have included such notes, replies to them are cited in the form 'see also', with no reference to the names of respondents. Local and church histories have been excluded, except in a few cases. Such histories are frequently invaluable for the genealogist, but there are far too many of them to be listed here. This is a bibliography of published works; hence the many manuscript works to be found in Oxford and London libraries are excluded.

One exclusion needs emphasis. My definition of Oxfordshire, for the purpose of this bibliography, excludes the University of Oxford and its colleges. Many works relating to the University are of genealogical interest, however, they concern the history of the nation as a whole, rather than just Oxfordshire. For example, many estate papers relating to property owned by the Colleges have been published—but the colleges owned properties in virtually every English county. Similarly, many monumental inscriptions from the Colleges have been published—but many of those commemorated were not connected with the county other than through the University. It is intended in due course to publish a bibliography solely devoted to works of genealogical interest concerning the universities of Oxford and Cambridge. The only works relating to Oxford University listed here are those which relate to the county as much as to the University.

Be warned—I cannot claim that this bibliography is comprehensive. Neither do I claim that it is totally accurate. Some works have been deliberately excluded. Others have undoubtedly been missed. If you come across anything that has been missed, please let me know, so that it can be included in a second edition in due course.

Most works listed here are readily available in the libraries listed below—although no library holds everything. Even if you are overseas, you should be able to find copies of the more important reference works in larger research libraries. However, some articles may prove difficult to locate—particularly articles in local periodicals. Never fear! Librarians are committed to making all publications universally available, and most public libraries are able to tap into the international inter-library loans system. Your local library should be able to borrow most of the items listed here, even if it has to go overseas to obtain them.

The work of compiling this bibliography has depended heavily on the resources of the libraries I have used. These included Exeter University Library, Exeter City Library, the Bodleian Library, the British Library and the Centre for Oxfordshire Studies. I am grateful to the librarians of all these institutions for their help. I am also grateful to Jill Muir and the Oxfordshire Family History Society for their encouragement, to Terry Humphries, who typed the manuscript, to Bob Boyd, who saw the book through the press, and to Jeremy Gibson, whose contributions are myriad! He loaned me his runs of a number of journals and read the first draft. His contribution is, however, much greater than that: his name appears as author on many of the more important works cited, and he was instrumental in founding a number of the more important journals—*O.F.H.* and *C.&Ch.* to name but two. Finally, a bibliography like this necessarily rests on the shoulders of its predecessors. The volumes by Cordeaux and Merry listed in section 2 below were indispensable in the work of compilation.

Stuart A. Raymond

LIBRARIES AND RECORD OFFICES

The major libraries and record offices concerned with Oxfordshire local studies are:

Centre for Oxfordshire Studies
Westgate
OXFORD, OX1 3BG

Bodleian Library
Broad Street
OXFORD, OX1 3BG

Oxfordshire Archives
County Hall
New Road
OXFORD, OX1 1ND

BIBLIOGRAPHIC PRESENTATION

Authors' names are in SMALL CAPITALS. Book and journal titles are in *italics*. Articles appearing in journals, and material such as parish register transcripts, forming only part of books are in inverted commas and textface type. Volume numbers are in **bold** and the individual number of the journal may be shown in parentheses. These are normally followed by the place of publication (except where this is London, which is omitted), the name of the publisher and the date of publication. In the case of articles, further figures indicate page numbers.

ABBREVIATIONS

B.B.O.A.J.	*Berks, Bucks and Oxon archaeological journal*
B.H.S.	*Banbury Historical Society*
C.&Ch.	*Cake and Cockhorse*
M.G.H.	*Miscellanea Genealogica et Heraldica*
N.S.	New Series
O.A.H.S.P.	*Oxfordshire Architectural and Historical Society proceedings*
O.A.S.	*Oxfordshire Archaeological Society [transactions and reports]*
O.F.H.	*Oxfordshire Family Historian*
O.H.S.	*Oxford Historical Society*
O.J.M.B.	*Oxford Journal of Monumental Brasses*
O.L.H.	*Oxfordshire Local Historian*
O.P.R.M.	*Oxfordshire parish registers: marriages*
O.R.S.	*Oxfordshire Record Society*
Ox.	*Oxoniensia*
P.P.R.S.	*Phillimore's Parish Register Series*

1. THE HISTORY OF OXFORDSHIRE

How did your ancestors live, work, eat and sleep? What was the world they lived in like? If you want to know the answer to questions like this, and to understand the world of parish registers, subsidy rolls and monumental brasses, you need to read up on local history. For Oxfordshire, a good beginning is provided by:

JESSUP, MARY. *A history of Oxfordshire*. Phillimore, 1975.

The authoritative work on the history of the county is:

The Victoria history of the counties of England: Oxfordshire. 11 vols. O.U.P. for the Institute of Historical Research, 1939-90. v.1. Includes Domesday book, political history, and schools, etc. v.2. Ecclesiastical history; social and economic history. v.3. The University of Oxford. v.4. The City of Oxford. v.5. Bullingdon Hundred. v.6. Ploughley Hundred. v.7. Dorchester and Thame Hundreds. v.8. Lewknor and Pyrton Hundreds. v.9. Bloxham Hundred. v.10. Banbury Hundred. v.11. Wootton Hundred (northern part). v.12. Wootton Hundred (South), including Woodstock. Further volumes in progress.

Parochial surveys, which include a limited amount of genealogical information, are included in:

BIRD, W. HOBART. *Old Oxfordshire churches*. Ed. J. Burrow & Co., 1932. With brief notes on brasses, etc.

SKELTON, J. *Skeltons engraved illustrations of the principal antiquities of Oxfordshire, from original drawings*. Oxford: J. Skelton, 1823.

A similar work for Northamptonshire includes many pedigrees and other genealogical information relating to North Oxfordshire families:

BAKER, GEORGE. *The history and antiquities of the county of Northampton*. 2 vols. John Bowyer Nichols & Son, 1822-30.

A number of works provide parochial surveys and similar works for areas smaller than the whole county:

KENNETT, WHITE. *Parochial antiquities attempted in the history of Ambrosden, Burcester and other adjacent parts in the counties of Oxford and Bucks*. New ed. 2 vols. Oxford: Clarendon Press, 1818. Includes many manorial documents.

BLOMFIELD, JAMES C. *History of the present Deanery of Bicester*. 8 pts. Oxford: Parker & Co., 1882-94. Parochial survey, giving manorial descents, lists of rectors, extracts from parish registers, churchwardens' accounts, etc.

DUNKIN, JOHN. *The history and antiquities of the hundreds of Bullingdon and Ploughley*. 2 vols. Harding, Mavor & Lepard, 1823. Parochial survey, including pedigrees, monumental inscriptions, lists of rectors, etc.

PEARMAN, M.T. 'Historical account of the Hundreds of Chiltern in Oxfordshire', *O.A.S.* **25**, 1890, 1-20.

WOOD, ANTHONY. *Survey of the antiquities of the city of Oxford*, ed. Andrew Clark. 3 vols. *O.H.S.* **15, 17 & 37**, 1889-99. v.1. The city and suburbs. v.2. Churches and religious houses. v.3. Addenda and indexes. A survey of the city written in 1661-6. The third volume includes many monumental inscriptions and excerpts from the parish register.

The history of Oxfordshire has been the subject of much research in recent years. Some interesting general works include:

EMERY, FRANK. *The Oxfordshire landscape*. Hodder and Stoughton, 1974.

MCKINLEY, ROBERT. *The surnames of Oxfordshire*. English surnames series **3**. Leopards Head Press, 1977. Discusses the origins of surnames; important for the genealogist. See also: POSTLES, DAVID. 'Nomina villanorum et burgensium: Oxfordshire bynames before c.1250', *Ox.* **54**, 1989, 319-25.

MARTIN, A.F., AND STEEL, R.W., eds. *The Oxford region: a scientific and historical survey*. Oxford: O.U.P., 1954.

The following titles are arranged chronologically:

ALLISON, K.J., BERESFORD, M.W., AND HURST, J.G., et al. 'The deserted villages of Oxfordshire', *Occasional paper* **17**. Leicester: University of Leicester Dept. of English Local History, 1965. Includes a gazetteer of deserted villages.

SCHUMER, BERYL. *The evolution of Wychwood to 1400: pioneers, frontiers and forests*. Dept. of English Local History Occasional papers, 3rd series **6**. Leicester: Leicester University Press, 1984.

HARVEY, P.D.A. *A medieval Oxfordshire village: Cuxham, 1240 to 1400*. O.U.P., 1965. Includes detailed list of manuscript sources for the history of Cuxham.

BUTCHER, A.F. 'Rent and the urban economy: Oxford and Canterbury in the later middle ages', *Southern history* **1**, 1979, 11-43. Based on tallage and rent rolls.

PRIOR, MARY. *Fisher Row: fishermen, bargemen and canal boatmen in Oxford, 1500-1900*. Oxford: Clarendon Press, 1982. Fascinating! The appendices include a summary account of the leases of Upper Fisher Row, 17-19th c., and detailed extracts from the census, 1841-71.

WALTER, JOHN. 'A 'rising of the people''? The Oxfordshire rising of 1596', *Past & present* **106**, 1985, 90-143.

VARLEY, FREDERICK JOHN. *The siege of Oxford during the Civil War, 1642-1646*. Oxford University Press, 1932.

ROBSON, R.J. *The Oxfordshire election of 1754: a study in the interplay of city, county and university politics*. O.U.P., 1949.

REANEY, B. *The class struggle in 19th century Oxfordshire: the social and communal background to the Otmoor disturbances of 1830 to 1835*. History workshop pamphlets **3**. Oxford: History Workshop, 1971.

TILLER, KATE, ed. 'Milton and Shipton in the 19th century', *Wychwoods history* **3**, 1987, 1-68.

HARRISON, B., AND TRINDER, B. *Drink and sobriety in an early Victorian country town: Banbury 1830-1860*. English historical review supplement **4**. Longmans, 1969.

MORGAN, D.H. *Harvesters and harvesting 1840-1900: a study of the rural proletariat*. Croom Helm, 1982. Primarily concerned with Berkshire, Buckinghamshire and Oxfordshire.

SAMUEL, RAPHAEL. 'Quarry roughs: life and labour in Headington Quarry 1860-1920: an essay in oral history', in his *Village life and labour*. Routledge & Kegan Paul, 1975, 139-263.

MILLER, CELIA, ed. *Rain and ruin: the diary of an Oxfordshire farmer, John Simpson Calvertt, 1875-1900*. Gloucester: Alan Sutton, 1983. Mentions many people from around Shipton under Wychwood.

WHITING, R.C. *The view from Cowley: the impact of industrialization upon Oxford, 1918-1939*. Oxford: Clarendon Press, 1983. Includes useful lit of archival sources.

This is very much a personal selection, merely intended to whet the appetite. There are numerous other county and local histories of Oxfordshire, many of which have genealogical value. A few are listed in the appropriate section below; for a reasonably comprehensive bibliography, see the volumes by Cordeaux and Merry identified below.

2. BIBLIOGRAPHY AND ARCHIVES

There are many excellent handbooks and bibliographies of value to the Oxfordshire genealogist. A good place to begin is:

BARRATT, D.M., AND VAISEY, D.G., eds. *Oxfordshire: a handbook for students of local history.* Oxford: Basil Blackwell for the Oxfordshire Rural Community Council, 1973.

More specifically for the genealogist is:

PILLING, JOHN. 'A guide to source materials for family historians in the Local Studies Library at Oxford Central Library', *O.F.H.* 5(2), 1989, 41-3. See also 5(5), 1990, 182-3.

The Oxfordshire researcher is fortunate in having a wide range of bibliographies available for consultation; they provide references to many more works—especially parish histories—than can be listed here. See:

CORDEAUX, E.H., AND MERRY, D.H. *A bibliography of printed works relating to Oxfordshire (excluding the University and city of Oxford).* O.H.S., N.S. 11, 1955. Supplementary volume, N.S. 28, 1981.

CORDEAUX, E.H., AND MERRY, D.H. *A bibliography of printed works relating to the City of Oxford.* O.H.S., N.S. 25, 1976.

CORDEAUX, E.H., AND MERRY, D.H. *A bibliography of printed works relating to the University of Oxford.* Oxford: Clarendon Press, 1968.

An earlier attempt to compile a genealogical bibliography for the county was made by:

TOMLINSON, STEVEN. 'A genealogical bibliography for Oxfordshire, Berkshire and Buckinghamshire', *O.F.H.* 1(5), 1978, 119-30. Not entirely superseded by the present work, as it lists a number of unpublished works and poll books which are excluded here.

General surveys of the extensive published literature on Banbury and Eynsham are provided by:

GIBSON, JEREMY. 'Tracing ancestors in Oxfordshire's second town: Banbury', *O.F.H.* 4(3), 1986, 70-76.

ATKINS, BRIAN. 'Eynsham bibliography: sources for the local historian', *Eynsham record* 1, 1984, 39-42; 2, 1985, 44-6.

CROSSLEY, ALAN. 'Eynsham: a suitable case for treatment', *Eynsham record* 1, 1984, 3-9. Discussion of sources available for the history of Eynsham.

A number of works list materials at Oxfordshire Record Office:

OXFORDSHIRE COUNTY RECORDS JOINT COMMITTEE. *The Oxfordshire County Record Office and its records.* Record publication 1. Oxford: the Committee, 1948. Reprinted with additions from *Ox.* 3, 1938, 111-22. Now outdated, but still useful.

Golden jubilee of the Oxfordshire County Record Office, 1935-85. Oxford: Oxfordshire County Council, 1985. Calendar of documents exhibited, including many of genealogical value.

OXFORDSHIRE COUNTY COUNCIL. COUNTY RECORDS JOINT COMMITTEE. *Report.* [Oxford: the Council], 1947-74. Includes list of accessions.

BOLTON, J.R., AND JONES, M., eds. *Summary catalogue of the privately deposited records in the Oxfordshire County Record Office.* Record publications 4. Oxford: Oxfordshire County Council, 1966.

BARNES, SHIRLEY. 'Genealogical sources in the Oxfordshire County Record Office', *O.F.H.* 1(5), 1978, 112-4.

Relevant contents of the Bodleian Library are also listed in a number of works:

BARRATT, D.M., AND VAISEY, D.G. *Material for Oxfordshire history in the Bodleian Library.* Oxford: Bodleian Library, 1974. General guide to both printed and manuscript material.

SPOKES, P.S. *Summary catalogue of manuscripts in the Bodleian Library relating to the city, county and university of Oxford: accessions from 1916 to 1962.* O.H.S., N.S. 17, 1964.

MADAN, F. *Rough list of manuscript materials relating to the history of Oxford contained in the printed catalogues of the Bodleian and college libraries.* Oxford: Clarendon Press, 1887.

Two articles provide general introductions to diocesan archives of interest to genealogists, although both are now rather out of date:

'Genealogical sources within the Diocese of Oxford', *O.F.H.* 1(1), 1977, 4-6. Brief discussion of parish registers, probate records, marriage bonds, etc.

PHILIP, I.G. 'Diocesan records in the Bodleian Library', *Genealogists magazine* 8(1), 1938, 7-9.

The Diocesan records are now in the Oxfordshire Archives. Further works on them are listed in section 12 below.

Two other works deserve notice here:

CLAPINSON, MARY. 'The topographical collections of Henry Hinton (1749-1816) and James Hunt (1795-1857)', *Ox.* 37, 1972, 215-20.

GIBSON, J.S.W. 'Strays in local record office collections', *O.F.H.* 3(3), 1983, 95-6. Lists material relating to Oxfordshire families in Staffordshire Record Office.

3. JOURNALS AND NEWSPAPERS

Genealogists should always subscribe to the journal of the family history society covering their area of interest. The best such journal that I have so far encountered is:

The Oxfordshire family historian: the journal of the Oxfordshire Family History Society. 1977-
Many of the articles in this journal are cited in this bibliography. It also contains many reports on projects such as the transcription of monumental inscriptions and the indexing of parish registers, together with other news—most of which I have not separately listed. Perhaps of most immediate use, however, are the many queries and expressions of interest from members, which may provide invaluable leads.

The most important historical journal for the county, containing many papers of genealogical interest, is:

Oxoniensia: a journal dealing with the archaeology, history and architecture of Oxford and its neighbourhood. Oxford: Oxfordshire Architectural and Historical Society, 1937-.

Other county wide journals include:

The Berks, Bucks & Oxon archaeological journal. 34 vols. Oxford: Berkshire Archaeological Society, 1889-1930. Continued by: *The Berkshire archaeological journal.* These are indexed in: BUNCE, F.M. 'Index of the Berks, Bucks and Oxon archaeological journal and of the Quarterly journal of the Berks Archaeological Society', *B.B.O.A.J.* 28(2), 1924, 1-24. Covers vols. 1-25, 1895-1919, of *B.B.O.A.J.* See also: 'The Berkshire archaeological journal: general index, volumes 26-50, 1920-1947', *Berkshire Archaeological journal* 52, 1950/51, 23-93.

Oxfordshire local history. Oxford: Oxfordshire Local History Association, 1980-

Top. Oxon: a bulletin of Oxfordshire local history. 22 issues. Oxford: Oxford Archaeological Society/Oxfordshire Rural Community Council, 1958-78. Contains brief historical notes and articles.

Oxfordshire Local History Association newsletter. Oxford: the Association, 1980-. For current information on Oxon local history events, projects, societies.

Proceedings of the Oxford Architectural and Historical Society. New series, 1860-1900.

Transactions of the Archaeological Society of North Oxfordshire. Banbury: the Society, 1853-5. Continued by: *Report of the Archaeological and Natural History Society of North Oxfordshire.* 1856-84. Continued by: *Oxfordshire Archaeological Society [transactions and reports].* 1888-1949. Indexed in 'Index to the transactions and reports', *O.A.S.* 61, 1915, 255-66.

The publications of record societies often contain works vital to the genealogist. Three series are published in Oxfordshire:

Oxfordshire Record Society. 1919-.

Oxford Historical Society. 1885-1936. N.S., 1939-.

Banbury Historical Society Records Section. 1959-.

Many individual record society volumes are listed below.

A number of Oxfordshire towns and villages have their own historical journals. They include:

Banbury

Cake & Cockhorse: the magazine of the Banbury Historical Society. Banbury: the Society, 1959-. A chronological list of articles is provided by: 'Cake and Cockhorse: the first quarter century', *C.&Ch.* 9(7), 1984, 205-20.

Eynsham

The Eynsham record: journal of the Eynsham History Group. Eynsham: the Group, 1984-.

Witney

Record of Witney. Witney: Witney & District Historical and Archaeological Society, 1977-. Originally entitled *Newsletter.*

Wychwood

Wychwood's history: the journal of the Wychwoods Local History Society. 1985-.

Newspapers often contain useful information. Those held at the Centre for Oxfordshire Studies are listed in:

'Local newspapers', *O.F.H.* 2(8), 1982, 250-51.

For extracts from the *Oxford Mercury* relating to Banbury, see:

GIBSON, J.S.W. 'A few weeks in 1795', *C.&Ch.* 11(4), 1989, 84-9.

An important unpublished index to an early newspaper is discussed by:

DAVIES, EILEEN. '*Jacksons Oxford journal* synopsis, 1753-1790', *O.F.H.* 1(9), 1979, 234-9.

4. GENEALOGICAL DIRECTORIES, BIOGRAPHICAL DICTIONARIES AND OCCUPATIONAL LISTS

A. *GENEALOGICAL DIRECTORIES*

Amongst the most valuable sources of genealogical information are the directories of members interests published by the various family history societies. These provide the names and addresses of their members, together with a list of surnames being researched. If yours is listed, maybe someone has already done all the work! Or at least, someone may be willing to share the labour. For Oxfordshire, see:

HOWARD-DRAKE, J.M. *Oxfordshire Family History Society directory of members interests, 1976-1987.* Oxford: the Society, 1987.

PERKINS, JOHN. *Oxfordshire families directory.* Oxford: Oxfordshire F.H.S., 1991.

B. *BIOGRAPHICAL DICTIONARIES*

Biographical dictionaries provide brief biographical information on the persons listed. Many are available; for general guidance on identifying them, see *English genealogy: an introductory bibliography.* Many dictionaries of occupational biography are listed in *Occupational sources for genealogists.* General works for Oxfordshire include:

TOYNBEE, MARGARET, AND YOUNG, PETER. *Strangers in Oxford: a side light on the first Civil War, 1642-1646.* Phillimore, 1973. Brief biographies of those resident in Oxford, with various lists.

GASKELL, E. *Oxfordshire leaders, social and political.* Queen Hithe Printing, [1900].

DALE, JOHN. *Oxfordshire and Berkshire historical descriptive and biographical in the reign of King Edward VII.* J.G. Hammond & Co., [190-].

GRANT, JOHN, ed. *Berkshire and Oxfordshire historical, biographical and pictorial.* London & Provincial Publishing Co., 1912. Biographies.

Who's who in Oxfordshire. Who's who in the Counties Series, 1936.

C. *OCCUPATIONAL SOURCES*

There are many works offering biographical information on persons of particular occupations. For a general listing of such works, see *Occupational sources for genealogists,* which complements the following list of Oxfordshire works. For clergymen, see section 12, for members of parliament and local government officials, section 14, for teachers and pupils, section 15.

Agricultural Labourers

HORN, PAMELA, ed. *Agricultural trade unionism in Oxfordshire, 1872-81.* O.R.S. **48**, 1974. Mainly minute book of Oxfordshire branches of the National Agricultural Labourers Union; many names.

Antiquarians

PANTIN, W.A. 'The Oxford Architectural and Historical Society, 1839-1939', *Ox.* **4**, 1939, 174-94. Includes lists of officers.

Apprentices

GIBSON, J.S.W. 'Some apprentices from eighteenth century Banbury', *C.&Ch.* **11**(1), 1988, 22-4. Gives brief biographical notices on Banbury boys apprenticed in Coventry, Warwickshire, and Oxford, 18th c.

GRAHAM, MALCOLM, ed. *Oxford city apprentices, 1697-1800.* O.H.S., N.S. **31**, 1987.

Architects

SAINT, ANDREW. 'Three Oxford architects', *Ox.* **35**, 1970, 53-102. Includes pedigree of Wilkinson, Rolfe and Moore, 18-19th c., with lists of the works of William Wilkinson, Harry Wilkinson Moore, and Clapton Crabb Rolfe—giving many names of those who commissioned them.

Bellringers

NICHOLS, NORA K. 'Did he ring a bell?', *O.F.H.* **4**(1), 1986, 15-16. See also **4**(3), 1986, 87-8. Includes list of 10 Oxford bell-ringers, 1734.

Blanket Weavers

PLUMMER, ALFRED, ed. *The Witney blanket industry: the records of the Witney blanket weavers.* George Routledge & Son, 1934. Includes many extracts from the 18th c. court books, with names.

Builders

HANSON, T.W. 'Halifax builders in Oxford', *Papers, reports, etc., read before the Halifax Antiquarian Society,* 1928, 253-317. Primarily concerned with Akroyd, Bentley and Hall families, 16-17th c., but includes accounts giving many other names.

JOPE, E.M. 'Abingdon Abbey craftsmen and building stone supplies', *Berkshire archaeological journal* **51**, 1948/9, 53-64. Many names, mainly from Taynton and Wheatley.

Canteen Staff

ADKINS, BARBARA. 'Banbury Rest Station & Canteen, 1914-19', *C.&Ch.* **8**(1), 1979, 13-16. Includes list of 'canteen helpers'.

Carpenters

GEE, E.A. 'Oxford carpenters, 1370-1530', *Ox.* **17/18**, 1952/3, 112-84. Identifies over 400 carpenters, and includes probate inventory of Robert Carow, 1531.

Carriers

JENKINS, STANLEY C. 'Witney carriers in 1903', *Record of Witney* **16**, [1983], 4-9. Includes list with residences.

Clockmakers

BEESON, C.F.C. *Clockmaking in Oxfordshire, 1400-1850.* 3rd ed. Oxford: Museum of the History of Science, 1989. Includes extensive biographical dictionary.

Convicts

INSELL, W.A. 'Ancestors in trouble', *O.F.H.* **2**(5 & 6), 1981, 137-42 & 188-95. Reviews sources for convicts.

GIBSON, J.S.W. 'Transported convicts' families in North Oxon', *O.F.H.* **2**(7), 1982, 216-7. See also **2**(8), 1982, 259-65; **3**(2), 1983, 38-41; **3**(3), 1983, 107-8 & **3**(4), 1984, 134. Includes list compiled in 1846.

Cordwainers

WILSON, J. 'The cordwainers and corvesors of Oxford', *Archaeological journal* **6**, 1849, 146-59 & 266-79. Includes 17th c. accounts, giving names.

Dancers

CHANDLER, KEITH. 'Assessing the evidence: a morris dance group', *O.F.H.* **3**(9), 1985, 290-92. Discusses evidence for 19th c. morris dancing, giving some names of dancers.

Enclosure Commissioners

TATE, W.E. 'Oxfordshire enclosure commissioners, 1737-1856', *Journal of modern history* **23**(2), 1951, 137-45. General discussion of the commissioners, with some names.

Excisemen

HOAD, JOYCE. 'Was your ancestor an excise man?', *O.F.H.* **5**, 1989-90, 84-6, 148-52 & 190-98.

Freemasons

HAWKINS, E.L. *A history of freemasonry in Oxfordshire.* Oxford: W.R. Bowden, 1882. Many names.

KERRY, A.J. *History of Freemasonry in Oxfordshire.* [Oxford?]: [ ], [1965].

TAUNT, HENRY W. *The official souvenir of the centenary of the Albion Lodge, Oxford, no.59, A[ncient] O[rder of] D[ruids], 1812-1912.* Oxford: Henry W. Taunt & Co., [1912]. Includes roll of honour, 1812-1912.

Golfers

OWEN, J.S.W. 'Banbury and District Golf Club, 1894-1919', *C.&Ch.* **11**(2), 1989, 30-42 & **11**(7), 1990, 154-73. Many names, including a list of members, 1914-15.

Innkeepers

BEESON, CYRIL FREDERICK CHERRINGTON. 'Seventeenth century inn-keepers in Banbury', *C.&Ch.* **1**, 1961, 122-5. Includes information from the parish register and other sources.

GIBSON, J.S.W. 'A century of tavern-keeping', *C.&Ch.* **7**(4), 1977, 103-15, & **8**(1), 1979, 3-12. Traces descent of the Unicorn and Three Tuns at Banbury, and includes pedigree of Stokes and Style families, 17-18th c.

LEEDS, E.T. '17th and 18th century wine-bottles of Oxford taverns', *Ox.* **6**, 1941, 44-55. Gives some names of innkeepers.

LAITHWATE, MICHAEL. 'The Reindeer Inn, Banbury', *C.&Ch.* **2**, 1962-5, 159-63. Includes names of owners, 17-19th c.

TAYLOR, ROYSTON. 'Innkeepers and victuallers in early seventeenth century Woodstock', *O.L.H.* **3**(6), 1991, 251-65. Includes list.

Masons

GEE, E.A. 'Oxford masons, 1370-1530', *Archaeological journal* **109**, 1952, 54-131. List with many biographical notes.

Photographers

GOSLING, SARAH. 'From daguerrotype to dry plate: the growth of professional photography in Banbury', *C.&Ch.* **9**(6), 1984, 158-64. Lists photographers.

Pillow Lace Makers

HORN, PAMELA L.R. 'Pillow lace-making in Victorian England: the experience of Oxfordshire', *Textile history* **3**, 1972, 100-115. Includes a bibliography noting sources which could be useful.

Pipemakers

KITCHENER, ROY. 'The clay tobacco pipe', *C.&Ch.* **4**, 1968-71, 196-203. Includes list of 67 pipemakers from the Banbury region (within 20-30 miles), 17-19th c.

Plush Manufacturers

HODGKINS, VERA, and BLOXHAM, CHRISTINE. *Banbury and Shutford plush*. Banbury: Banbury Museum/Banbury Historical Society, 1980. Reprints a history of the Wrench family, 1747-1947, and includes notes on many plush manufacturers, late 18th c., especially the Newman family.

Policemen

CARLTON, EILEEN. 'Thomas Savings, Eynsham's police constable 1863-1871', *Eynsham record* 3, 1986, 27-30. Illustrates the use of police records as biographical and genealogical sources.

WILLIAMS, MYRA. 'A police ancestor in nineteenth century Banbury', *O.F.H.* 4(4), 1987, 123-6. Tustin family; illustrates use of police records.

Potters

'Witney and the seventeenth century pewter industry', *Record of Witney* 6, 1979, 9-12. Includes lists of potters at Oxford, Chipping Norton, Witney, Banbury, Thame, Faringdon and Woodstock.

Servants

PARRY, COLIN J. 'Missing from home, part 3: in service', *F.T.M.* 3(12), 1987, 13. Includes extracts from the 1851 census for servants at Blenheim Palace, Woodstock, and Magdalen College, Oxford University.

Shareholders

POTTS, A. 'Ernest Samuelson and the Britannia works', *C.&Ch.* 4, 1968-71, 187-93. Includes lists of shareholders in Samuelson & Co. in 1889 and 1905, many of them from Banbury.

Soldiers and Militiamen

Many men of Oxfordshire served in the army, or in the militia, and much information on them is available in the various regimental histories, etc., which have been compiled. These cannot all be listed here. The works listed below include only those publications which provide lists of officers and men, and which may, therefore, be of direct interest to the genealogist. It is arrange in rough chronological order.

VARLEY, F.J. 'Oxford army list for 1642-1646', *Ox.* 2, 1937, 141-51.

NEWBOLT, SIR HENRY. *The story of the Oxfordshire and Buckinghamshire Light Infantry (the old 43rd and 52nd Regiments)*. Country Life & George Newnes, 1915. Includes list of officers and men 1914-15. The volume commences in 1741.

MOORSOM, W.S., ed. *Historical record of the Fifty Second Regiment (Oxfordshire Light Infantry) from the year 1755 to the year 1858*. Richard Bentley, 1860. Includes many names.

WILLAN, F. *History of the Oxfordshire Regiment of Militia (fourth battalion Oxfordshire Light Infantry), 1778-1900, including the diary of Thomas Mosley Crowder, 1852-1885*. Oxford: Horace Hart, 1900. Includes list of officers, 1778-1899.

WILLIAMS, J. ROBERT. 'Oxfordshire veterans of the 30th Foot', *O.F.H.* 3(3), 1983, 94-5. List 1806-28.

WILLIAMS, J. ROBERT. 'Oxfordshire out-pensioners from the 52nd Foot', *O.F.H.* 3(1), 1983, 27-9. Includes list, 1806-38.

WILLIAMS, J. ROBERT. 'Oxfordshire volunteers in the Napoleonic wars', *O.F.H.* 3(4), 1984, 117-20. Includes notes on paylists at the Public Record Office, including a transcript of that for the company of Pyrton Hundred, 1804-5.

[GIBSON, J.S.W.] *Oxfordshire militia ballot 1831: City of Oxford; Hundreds of Bullingdon, Thame and Dorchester*. Oxford: Oxfordshire Family History Society, 1989.

GIBSON, JEREMY. 'A quasi census for Oxford and the Hundreds of Bullingdon, Dorchester and Thame', *O.F.H.* 5(3), 1989, 86-9. Discusses separately published militia list of 1831.

WINSTON, JOHN, AND FANE, JOHN WILLIAM. *Oxfordshire militia: sketch of the history of the regiment*. Oxford: E.W. Morris, 1869. Includes list of officers, 1869.

MOCKLER-FERRYMAN, A.F., ed. *The Oxfordshire Light Infantry in South Africa: a narrative of the Boer War*. Eyre and Spottiswoode, 1901. Includes various lists of names.

Soldiers died in the Great War 1914-19, part 47: The Oxfordshire and Buckinghamshire Light Infantry. H.M.S.O., 1921. Reprinted Polstead: J.B. Hayward & Son, 1989.

KEITH-FALCONER, A. *The Oxfordshire Hussars in the Great War (1914-1918)*. John Murray, 1927. Includes various lists of officers and men.

Soldiers and Militiamen *continued*

WHEELER, C. *Memorial record of the Seventh (service) battalion the Oxfordshire and Buckinghamshire Light Infantry.* Oxford: Basil Blackwell, 1921. Includes various lists of officers and men, 1914-19.

The Oxfordshire and Buckinghamshire Light Infantry. [ ]: [ ], [1919?]. Roll of honour, 1914-19.

The Oxfordshire and Buckinghamshire Light Infantry. [ ]: [ ], c.1945. Roll of honour, 1939-45.

BROOME, JACQUI. 'The roll of honour 1939-45', *Record of Witney* 9, 1980, 7-8. Witney soldiers.

BINT, R. *1940-1944 record of service: the Highlands Platoon (East Company) 6th Oxfordshire (Oxf. city) battalion, Home Guard.* Oxford: [ ], 1945.

Swan Owners

TICEHURST, N.F. 'The swan-marks of Oxfordshire and Buckinghamshire', *O.A.S.* **82**, 1936, 97-130. Lists 175 swan owners, 16th c.

Tradesmen

'The Banbury trades index', *C.&Ch.* **9**(5), 138. Discussion of an index housed at Banbury Museum.

MILNE, J.G. *Catalogue of Oxfordshire seventeenth century tokens.* Oxford: O.U.P., 1935. See also *Ox.* **10**, 1945, 104-5. Includes biographical notices of many issuers.

LEEDS, E. THURLOW, ed. 'Oxford tradesmens tokens', *O.A.S.* **75**, 1923, 355-498. Gives many biographical notes on tradesmen.

CHINNOR HISTORICAL AND ARCHAEOLOGICAL SOCIETY. *Seventeenth century tradesmen's tokes with particular reference to Chinnor.* Occasional paper **6**. Chinnor: the Society, [198-].

SUMNER, MARY. 'Tradesmen of Hook Norton in the nineteenth century', *C.&Ch.* **9**(3), 1983, 74-8. Useful discussion of sources.

5. VISITATION RETURNS, PEDIGREES, ETC.

In the sixteenth and seventeenth centuries, the heralds undertook 'visitations' of the counties to determine the rights of gentry to bear heraldic arms. One consequence of this activity was the compilation of pedigrees of most leading families. Many pedigrees from Oxfordshire visitations have been printed; see:

TURNER, WILLIAM HENRY, ed. *The visitations of the county of Oxford taken in the years 1566 by William Harvey, Clarencieux; 1574 by Richard Lee, Portcullis; and in 1634 by John Philpott, Somerset, and William Ryly, Bluemantle, deputies of Sir John Borrough, Kt., Garter, and Richard St.George, Kt., Clarencieux, together with the Gatherings of Oxfordshire collected by Richard Lee in 1574.* Harleian Society **5**, 1871.

PHILLIPPS, SIR T., ed. *Visitations of Oxfordshire, 1574 and 1634.* Middle Hill: Typis Medio-Montanis, 184-.

'Oxfordshire visitation by Lee in 1574', *Topographer* **5**, 1790, 14-53.

'Pedigrees from the visitation of Oxfordshire, 1634', *M.G.H.* 4th series **5**, 1913, 97-104, 141-9, 193-200 & 254-60. 34 pedigrees.

'Visitation of Oxfordshire, 1668-9', *M.G.H.* 5th series **1**, 1916, 311; **2**, 1916-17, 121, 161, 201, 241 & 281; **3**, 1918-19, 2-3 & 83. 9 pedigrees.

An early 19th century collection of pedigrees is printed in:

PHILLIPPS, T. *Oxfordshire pedigrees from no.1557 Harl.MSS.* [Middle Hill: Typis Medio-Montanis, 18—?]. Includes pedigrees of Cobb of Alderbury, Bethome of Adwell, Ashcombe of Alvescot, Barber of Adderbury, Danvers of Adderbury, Jones of Asthall, Kenion of Astholl, Denton of Ambroseden and Doyly of Adderbury.

A number of works provide either pedigrees, biographical notes, or indexes to sources, for families from particular places. These are listed here.

Begbroke
See Kidlington

Burford
MOODY, R.A. 'Burford families', *O.F.H.* **1**(5), 1978, 131. Discusses the author's card index to records of Burford families.

Emmington
DAVIS, J.W. 'Emmington families', *O.F.H.* **1**(3), 1977, 63-5. List of Emmington and Chinnor families for whom the Chinnor Historical and Archaeological Society have compiled notes.

Enstone

JORDAN, JOHN. *A parochial history of Enstone in the county of Oxford, being an attempt to exemplify the compilation of parish histories from antiquarian remains, ecclesiastical structures and monuments, ancient and modern documents, manorial records, parish registers and account books, &c, &c.* John Russell Smith, 1857. Includes many extracts from original documents, and notices of many Enstone families, especially Lee and Dillon.

Kidlington

STAPLETON, MRS. BRYAN. *Three Oxfordshire parishes: a history of Kidlington, Yarnton and Begbroke.* O.H.S. **24**, 1893. Includes numerous pedigrees and extracts from original documents, including Kidlington marriages, 1574-1754.

Kingham

MANN, RALPH. 'Kingham families', *O.F.H.* **1**(3), 66-7. Lists families from Kingham for whom the author has compiled pedigrees.

Mapledurham

COOKE, A.H. *The early history of Mapledurham.* O.R.S. **7**, 1925. Includes medieval court rolls, pedigree of Blount, list of vicars, histories of the Warenne, De Gournay, Bardolf, Lynde and Iwardby families, etc.

Standlake

'Standlake pedigrees', *O.F.H.* **1**(3), 1977, 62. List of pedigrees compiled by Mrs. Goadby for families from Standlake.

Witney

'Victorian Witney and its families', *Record of Witney* **8**, 1981, 1-30. Includes notes on many families, with 18-19th c. pedigrees of Wilkinson, Batt, Leigh, Early, Smith and Wright, and a roll of honour of soldiers who fell 1914-19.

6. FAMILY HISTORIES

A considerable amount of research on Oxfordshire families has been completed, and is listed here. Many of these works include information on related families; even if your surname is not directly mentioned below, information on the family may well be included in some of the works cited. Biographies are generally not included here; they may be identified by consulting the bibliographies of Cordeaux and Merry listed in section 2. Works which have been completed but not published are also excluded.

Addington

BELFIELD, E.M.G. *The annals of the Addington family.* Winchester: Warren, 1959. 15-20th c. Of Fringford, Oxfordshire, and Potterspury, Northamptonshire.

Allnutt

NOBLE, ARTHUR. *The families of Allnutt and Allnatt.* Aylesbury: Dolphin, 1962. Oxfordshire, Buckinghamshire, Berkshire, etc., 16-20th c. Includes pedigrees and wills.

Apletree

APLETREE, REGINALD A. 'The Apletrees (or Appletree) in Banbury', *C.&Ch.* **11**(5), 1990, 110-11. 17-19th c.

Arsic

MORIARTY, G. ANDREWS. 'The Barony of Coggs', *O.A.S.* **75**, 1930, 309-20. Arsic family; includes pedigree, 12-13th c.

Austin

'Austin: memoranda relating to the Austin family, from the *Booke of Common Prayer* and the *Holy Bible ...*', *M.G.H.* N.S. **1**, 1874, 340. Sibford Ferris, 17-18th c.

Babington

C., G.T. 'Inedited additions to the pedigree of Babington', *Topographer & genealogist* **1**, 1846, 133-41, 259-79 & 333-43. See also 396.

Badgers

See Pointer

Bainbridge

See Wickson

Barefoot

BAREFOOT, MICHAEL. 'The wandering Barefoots of Iffley', *O.F.H.* **4**(1), 1986, 14-15. See also **4**(2), 1986, 64. 18-19th c.

Family Histories continued

Barentine
LAMBORN, E.A. GREENING. 'History of Parliament: the Barentines', *Notes & queries* **183**, 1942, 190-92. See also 350-1. Barentine family; medieval.
'Descent of the family of Barentyne in Oxfordshire to the year 1485', *O.A.S.* **55**, 1909, 30-32.

Barnes
BARNES, ANDREW. 'Research on a common surname', *O.F.H.* **4**(3), 1986, 77-8. Barnes family, 18-19th c.

Bartlett
TAYLOR, E. BARTLETT. 'The Bartlett family, carpenters and builders', *Record of Witney* **19**, 1985, 14-20. 16-19th c., includes pedigree.

Bayley
HORTON-SMITH, LIONEL GRAHAM HORTON. 'The Bayley family of Dorset, Somerset, Oxon and Berks', *Notes & queries for Somerset & Dorset* **25**(234), 1947, 41-9. Reprinted Sherborne: Sawtells, 1947. 16-17th c.

Beazley
See Byseley

Bedding
BEDDING, DOROTHY. 'The Beddings of North Leigh', *O.F.H.* **3**(7), 244-6. 19-20th c.

Beesley
ADKINS, BARBARA. 'The Beesley family of Alcester and Banbury', *C.&Ch.* **8**(7), 1981, 189-202. Includes pedigrees 17-19th c.
EDMONDS, JOSEPHINE. 'The search for Alfred Beesley', *O.F.H.* **4**(7), 1988, 223-9. Beesley and Reynolds families, 17-19th c.

Bisley
See Byseley

Bliss
EVANS, R.LL. 'The Bliss mills and the Bliss family in Chipping Norton, 1758-1920', *Top. Oxon* **20**, 1975, 6-12.

Blount
BROOKS, E.ST.J. 'Sir Thomas Blount, executed in 1400, and the Blounts of Kingston Blount', *M.G.H.* 5th series **7**, 1929-31, 73-83, 114-9, 158-76, 215-22, 254-74 & 315-25. See also 120-24.

Bolton
See Franklyn

Boteler
See Danvers

Bowerman
SHEEHAN, ELAINE. 'Three Bowerman brothers from Oxfordshire', *O.F.H.* **4**(5), 1987, 145-8. Early 19th c. convicts in Australia.

Boxe
PEARSE, WENDY. 'Leonard Boxe, gentleman of Ascott', *Wychwoods history* **6**, 1991, 19-29. Includes pedigree 17th c.

Brakspear
SHEPPARD, FRANCIS. *Brakspear's Brewery, Henley on Thames, 1779-1979*. Henley: the Brewery, 1979. The Brakspear family have run the Brewery for 200 years.

Bricknell
See Skillicorne

Bull
BULL, JOSEPH CECIL. *Miscellaneous notes, pedigrees, etc., relating to persons of the surname of Bull*. St.Catherine Press, 1911. Banbury area; includes pedigrees and numerous extracts from parish registers, feet of fines, wills, etc.

Bush
See Gill

Byseley
BEAZLEY, FRANK C. *Pedigree of Byseley, Bisley or Beazley of Newington and Warborough, Co.Oxon, Ryde and Alverstoke, Co.Southampton, and Oxton, Co.Chester.* Mitchell, Hughes and Clarke, 1928. Reprinted from *M.G.H.* 5th series, **6**, 1928. 16-20th c.

Calcutt
SCHUMER, BERYL PHYLLIS. *The Calcutts of North Leigh, Oxfordshire: a report to Australian descendants.* 2 pts. Melbourne: the author, 1970. 16-20th c., includes pedigrees.

Carter
PAUL, E.D. 'The papers of Richard Carter, esq', *Ox.* **32**, 1967, 74-77. Papers of an 18th c. justice and lawyer.

Chamberlain
See Danvers

Chaundy
ADKINS, BARBARA A. 'The Chaundy family in Oxford', *O.F.H.* **3**(8), 1985, 259-60. 16-19th c.
ADKINS, BARBARA A. 'Oh, to have a convict ancestor', *O.F.H.* **4**(8), 1988, 243-6. Chaundy family, 19th c.

Cheney

John Cheney and his descendants: printers in Banbury since 1767. Banbury: Cheney & Sons, 1936. Includes folded pedigree, 18-20th c.

CHENEY, C.R. 'Cheney & Sons: two centuries of printing in Banbury', *C.&Ch.* **3**, 1965-8, 167-75. 18-20th c. family and its business.

LAMBORN, E.A. GREENING. 'The *Complete peerage* and *The history of Parliament*', *Notes & queries* **188**, 1945, 11-12. Inaccuracies in major works relating to the Cheney family.

Churchill

GREEN, DAVID. *The Churchills of Blenheim.* Constable, 1984. 17-20th c., includes pedigree. See also Spencer-Churchill.

ROWSE, A.L. *The early and the later Churchills.* Reprint Society, 1959. Also published separately as *early* and *later*; Dorset and Blenheim.

Clifford

CLIFFORD, HUGH. *The house of Clifford from before the Conquest.* Phillimore, 1988.

The Clifford Association newsletter. Crawley: D.J.H. Clifford, 1983-.

Cobb

COBB, DAVID. 'A tree full of trusties', *O.F.H.* **5**(4), 1990, 135-43. Cobb family, 18-19th c.

Cole

LOFTUS, E.A. *A history of the descendants of Maximilian Cole of Oxford, who flourished in the 17th century.* Adlard & Son, 1938. Oxfordshire and London; includes folded pedigree in pocket.

Cope

GIBSON, J.S.W. 'Heraldry, horology, and horticulture at Hanwell', *C.&Ch.* **11**(1), 1988, 17-20. Funeral certificates of Sir William Cope, 1637, and Sir Anthony Cope, 1675.

JAKEMAN, CLARE. 'Cofferer Cope and the Copes of Canons Ashby', *C.&Ch.* **9**(5), 1984, 166-7. 16th c.

Cornewall

READE, COMPTON. 'The Cornewalls of Burford', *Genealogical magazine* **7**, 1904, 22-7, 80-83 & 97-101. Medieval-18th c.

Cotton

CRAY, JUNE. 'Family reconstitution: the Cotton and Messenger families in Thame, 1600-1665', *O.L.H.* **3**(4), 1990, 166-8.

Croeker

'Confirmation of arms by William Hervy, Norroy, to John Croeker of Hoeknorton, dated 1556', *M.G.H.* **1**, 1868, 140-41. Hook Norton.

Croke

CROKE, SIR A. *The genealogical history of the Croke family, originally named Le Blount.* 2 vols. John Murray, 1823. Le Blount of Ixworth, Suffolk; Croke of Oxfordshire, etc., medieval-19th c.

Currill

DYE, BARBARA. 'The Currills of Oxfordshire', *O.F.H.* **4**(4), 1987, 128-9. 19-20th c.

Curson

COKAYNE, G.E. 'Pedigree of Curson of Waterperry, Co.Oxford', *M.G.H.* 3rd series **1**, 1896, 209-17. See also **2**, 1898, 80, & **3**, 1900, 127. 16-18th c., includes extracts from parish registers and monumental inscriptions.

Danvers

MACNAMARA, F.N. *Memorials of the Danvers family (of Dauntsey and Culworth): their ancestors and descendants from the Conquest till the termination of the eighteenth century, with some account of the alliances of the family and of the places where they were seated.* Hardy & Page, 1895. Includes medieval pedigree of Danvers of Buckinghamshire, Berkshire and Oxfordshire, etc.

P. 'Extracts from a volume of Robert Aske's collections, marked with a cinquefoil, written in the reign of Henry VIII, [Pt.4]: Pedigree of Danvers of Cotherop, Co.Oxon, including descents of Umpton, Englefield, Tracy, Gate, Fray, Walgrave, Power, Langstone, Boteler, Gifford, Fowler, Chamberlain, &c., &c.', *Collectanea topographica et genealogica* **1**, 1834, 324-30.

Dashwood

TOWNSEND, JAMES. *The Oxfordshire Dashwoods.* Oxford: O.U.P., 1922. 17-20th c., includes short folded pedigree.

Davey

DAVEY, E.C. *Memoirs of an Oxfordshire old Catholic family and its connections from 1566 to 1897.* Vail & Co., 1897. Davey family; includes extracts from the Britwell Roman Catholic register, 1765-88.

Davis

REEVES, IVY. 'The family of John Davis, bargeman', *Journal of the Henley-on-Thames Archaeological & Historical Group* 7, 1989, 21-2.

Deely

ADKINS, BARBARA. '17th century marriage tangles', *O.F.H.* 4(1), 1986, 5-7. Deely family.

Donne

DAVIDSON, ALAN. 'An Oxford family: a footnote to the life of John Donne', *Recusant history* 13, 1976, 299-300. 16th c.

Dormer

MACLAGAN, MICHAEL. 'The family of Dormer in Oxfordshire and Buckinghamshire', *Ox.* 11, 1946-7, 90-101. Includes pedigree, 16-18th c.

D'Oyly

BAYLEY, WILLIAM D'OYLY. *A biographical, historical, genealogical and heraldic account of the house of D'Oyly*. John Bowyer Nichols & Son, 1845. Medieval-19th c., of various counties, including Oxfordshire.

BAYLEY, W.D. 'Pedigree of the early D'Oylys', *Topographer & genealogist* 1, 1846, 366-78.

Druce

DRUCE, FRANCES. 'The Druce family of Goring, Oxfordshire', *O.F.H.* 4(3), 1986, 79-81. 17-19th c.

DRUCE, C. *A genealogical account of the family of Druce of Goreing in the county of Oxon, and those of kin to the children of George Druce, citizen and painter-stainer of the parish of All Saints, Breadsteet, in the city of London, by whom this genealogy was taken* ... London: [ ], 1735. 17-18th c. Goring.

Early

PLUMMER, ALFRED, AND EARLY, RICHARD E. *The blanket makers, 1669-1969: a history of Charles Early & Marriott (Witney) Ltd.* Routledge & Kegan Paul, 1969. Includes pedigrees of the Early family, 16-20th c., and of the Marriott family, 18-20th c.

Elkington

ADAMS, A. *The Elkington family in England and America, being the ancestry and descendants of George Elkington of Burlington County, New Jersey*. Hartford, Conn: privately printed, 1945. Elkington of Cropredy and Mollington; Woodhull of Mollington; Hall and Rede families of Swerford.

Englefield

See Danvers

Eustace

EUSTACE, DONALD W. *The Eustaces of the Chiltern Hundreds*. 2 vols. The author, 1974-9. Medieval-20th c. Oxfordshire, Berkshire, Buckinghamshire, etc.

Evans

See Wickson

Fardon

BROWN-GRANT, EVELYN. 'John Fardon: clockmaker and amateur horticulturalist', *O.F.H.* 3(4), 1984, 127-30, & 3(5), 1984, 148-9. 18-19th c.

BROWN-GRANT, EVELYN. 'A clockmaking family', *O.F.H.* 3(6), 1984, 208-11. See also 3(7), 1985, 235-6. Fardon family, 18-20th c.

Fettiplace

DUNLOP, J. RENTON. 'The family of Fettiplace', *M.G.H.* 5th series 2, 1916-17, 93-100, 131-3, 183-92, 202-10, 242-56 & 282-92. Berkshire, Oxfordshire and Gloucestershire; pedigree, 13-20th c.

Fiennes

FIENNES, D.M. 'A study in family relationships: William Fiennes and Margaret Wykeham', *C.&Ch.* 8(2), 1980, 27-45. 15th c.

DAVIDSON, ALAN. 'The Fiennes family and founders' kin', *Notes & queries* 220, 1975, 294. 16th c.

FIENNES, DAVID. 'A study in family relationships: William Fiennes (d.1471) and Margaret Wykeham his wife (d.1477)', *O.F.H.* 2(1), 1980, 5-23.

FIENNES, DAVID. 'The owner of Broughton Castle in 1729', *C.&Ch.* 4, 1968-71, 147-57. Includes pedigrees showing relationship of Fiennes and Twisleton, 16-18th c.

Fowler

CARTER, WILLIAM F. 'The Fowlers of Hambleton', *Genealogist* 7, 1883, 4-10. Hambleton, Rutland; also of Oxfordshire, Bedfordshire and Buckinghamshire. Includes wills, 16-17th c.
See also Danvers

Franklyn

FRANKLYN, CHARLES A.H. *A short genealogical & heraldic history of the families of Frankelyn of Kent and Franklyn of Antigua and Jamaica, B.W.I., together with sections on the families of Bolton of Sandford and Gray of Billericay.* Edward O. Beck, 1932. Sandford, Oxfordshire; Billericay, Essex. 16-20th c.

Fray

See Danvers

Frederick

SUCKLING, F.H. *The family of Frederick of Frederick Place, Old Jewry, London, and of Bampton, Oxon.* Exeter: William Pollard, 1911. 17-18th c.

Gainsford

GAINSFORD, WILLIAM DUNN, ed. *Annals of the house of Gainsford, sometimes of the counties of Surrey, Oxon, Monmouth, Nottingham, Lincoln & Kent between the years A.D. 1331 and A.D. 1909.* Horncastle: W.K. Morton & Sons, 1909. Includes pedigrees and many extracts from original sources.

Garrett

See Taunton

Gate

See Danvers

Giffard

MORIARTY, G. ANDREWS. 'South Newington and the Giffards', *Genealogists magazine* 6, 1932-4, 282-5. Medieval.

Gifford

See Danvers and Tusmore

Gilkes

DIX-HAMILTON, M.L. 'Gilkes of Sibford: an enterprising yeoman family', *C.&Ch.* 3, 1965-8, 59-64. 16-20th c.

Gill

An old Oxford business, 1680-1926. Oxford: Gill & Co., 1926. Brief history of Gill & Co. Ltd., ironmongers, with notes on Smythe, Bush, Ward, Pitcher and Gill.

Gillett

TAYLOR, AUDREY M. *Gilletts, bankers at Banbury and Oxford: a study in local economic history.* Oxford: Clarendon Press, 1964. Includes pedigree of Gillett, 18-20th c.

Gillett *continued*

TAYLOR, AUDREY. 'The Gilletts in Banbury and Oxford: a study in local history', *C.&Ch.* 1, 1959-62, 74-6. 19th c.

Glynne

WHITTAKER, W.E.B. 'Glynne of Bicester and Hawarden', *Genealogical magazine* 7, 1904, 64-72. 17-19th c. Hawarden, Flintshire.

Golden

HORTON-SMITH, L. GRAHAM H. 'The Goldens of Ensham, Co.Oxon', *Genealogical quarterly* 3(1), 1934, 38-47. 18-19th c. Actually Eynsham.

Goodwin

'Pedigree of Goodwin of Alkerton and Epwell, Oxfordshire', *M.G.H.* 4th series 2, 1908, 150-52 & 190-95. 16-17th c., includes parish register extracts.

'Pedigree of Goodwin of Horley, Oxfordshire', *M.G.H.* 4th series 2, 1908, 32-8. 16-18th c.

Gray

See Franklyn

Grosvenor

See Taunton

Haines

See King

Hall

WHITE, GILL, AND WILLIAMSON, JEAN. 'The Halls of Hook Norton: carpenters, wheelwrights and well sinkers', *C.&Ch.* 9(3), 1983, 79-85. Includes pedigree, 18-19th c.
See also Elkington

Harcourt

HARCOURT, EDWARD WILLIAM, ed. *The Harcourt papers.* 14 vols. Oxford: James Parker & Co., [1876-1905]. 18th c. letters and memoirs, with pedigree and genealogical information from the medieval period onwards.

Harwell

FLETCHER, JOHN, AND WHITTAKER, JAN. *The Harwell trail.* Abingdon: J.M. Fletcher, 1981. Includes pedigrees, 13-20th c.

Hawtin

The Hawtayne heritage: newsletter of the Hawtin family. Leeds: M. Hawtin, 1987-.

Hayes

Proceedings of the Bicentennial gathering of the descendants of Henry Hayes at Unionville, Chester County, Pa., September 2nd 1905, together with a partial genealogy and other material relating to the family. West Chester, Pa: Committee for the Family, 1906. Originally an Oxfordshire family.

Hemming

BARNARD, E.A.B. *The Hemmings of Alcester and Oxford: an old-time family correspondence, 1791-1819.* Evesham: W. & H. Smith, 1931. Alcester, Warwickshire.

Hercy

HERSEY, CHAS. JAS. 'Hercy of Nettlebed, Oxon', *M.G.H.* 3rd series 5, 1904, 316-7. Pedigree, 16-19th c.

Heylyn

See Trinder

Higgins

PAINTIN, H. *An old Oxford family, 1572-1919.* Oxford: Hall the Printer, 1919. Reprinted from the *Oxford journal.* Higgins family, 17-20th c.

Higgs

HIGGS, WILLIAM MILLER. *A history of the Higges or Higgs family of South Stoke, in the county of Oxford, and of Thatcham in the county of Berks* ... Adlard & Son, 1933. Includes many pedigrees, wills, list of Chancery proceedings, and apprenticeship indentures, etc., etc.

Hord

E., W.S. 'Pedigree of the family of Hord, of Salop, Oxon and Surrey', *Topographer & genealogist* 1, 1846, 33-42.

Horniman

SHAW, HERBERT. 'The Hornimans and Smiths of Witney', *Record of Witney* 9, 1980, 4-6. 19-20th c.

Iving

YURDAN, MARILYN. *A guide to family history.* Hornchurch: Ian Henry, 1985. Despite the title, this is really an account of how the author researched the Iving family of West Oxfordshire.

Jackson

'Jackson family', *M.G.H.* N.S. 4, 1884, 314-5. Cuddesdon; extract from family bible, 17-18th c.

James

See Wickson

Johnson

DRINKWATER, P. *The Johnsons of Tidmington.* Shipton on Stour: the author, 1979? Tidmington, Warwickshire. Originally of Burford.

King

KING, RUFUS. 'Extracts from English parish registers relating to King and Haines families', *New England historical and genealogical register* 43, 1889, 256-7. Somerset and Oxfordshire; 16-17th c.

Kinman

KEEGAN, PAMELA. 'The Kinmans and Cooks of Cropredy (1775-1884)', *C.&Ch.* 7(8), 1979, 251-6. 18-19th c.

Knibb

LEE, RONALD A. *The Knibb family, clockmakers.* Byfleet: Manor House Press, 1964. 17-18th c.

Knollys

KNOLLYS, W. *Some remarks on the claim to the Earldom of Banbury, ...* J. Andrews, 1835. Knollys family.

PEARMAN, M.T. 'Sir Francis Knollys', *Genealogist* N.S. 1, 1884, 139-44.

PEARMAN, M.T. 'The Banbury peerage', *Genealogist* N.S. 1, 1884, 42-5. Knollys family, 17th c.

JONES, T.W. 'The Knolles or Knollys family of Rotherfield Greys, Oxfordshire: Mrs Lettice Knolles nee Pennyston, her parentage, family connections and subsequent marriage', *Herald & genealogist* 8, 1874, 289-302. 15-16th c.

PARMITER, GEOFFREY DE C. 'The Countess of Banbury and her sons', *C.&Ch.* 8(4), 1980, 86-96. Knollys family, 17th c.

The petition of William, Earl of Banbury to His Majesty claiming the Earldom of Banbury, with His Majesty's reference thereof to the House of peers and the report of His Majesty's Attorney General annexed. [By authority], 1808. Knollys family; includes pedigree, 17-18th c.

Langstone

See Danvers

Lee

LEE, FREDERICK GEORGE. 'Pedigree of the family of Lee, Co's Chester, Bucks, and Oxon', *M.G.H.* 2nd series 1, 1886, 101-8, 127-32 & 147-8. 14-19th c.

Family Histories continued

Lee continued

LEE, RUPERT HENRY MELVILLE. *Related to Lee*. 3 pts. Oxford: the author, 1963-4. Medieval-20th c., of Buckinghamshire, Oxfordshire, Cheshire, etc.
See also Wilmot

Leigh

F[IENNES], D.E.M. 'Gossip column', *C.&Ch.* 8(4), 1980, 97-8. Includes pedigree of Leigh, 17-19th c., showing relationship with Twisleton.

Lenthall

PAINTIN, HARRY. *Burford Priory and its association with the Lenthall family; also a brief account of the church and parish of Besselsleigh*. Oxford: Oxford Times, 1907. Besselsleigh, Berkshire. 15-18th c.

Loveday

MARKHAM, SARAH. *John Loveday of Caversham, 1711-1789: the life and tours of an eighteenth-century onlooker*. Salisbury: Michael Russell, 1984. Includes pedigree, 17-19th c.

Lydall

LYDALL, EDWARD. *Lydall of Uxmore*. [ ], 1980. Includes pedigrees, 16-19th c.

Marmion

WRIGHT, HILARY. 'The Marmions of Adwell', *Top. Oxon* 17, 1971, 5-8. Includes pedigree, 15-16th c.

Marriott
See Early

Marshall

PAUL, D. 'The Marshall family', *Top. Oxon* 15, 1970. Brief note, 17-20th c.

Mawle

ADKINS, BARBARA. 'The Mawle family, ironmongers and mayors of Banbury', *C.&Ch.* 7(5), 1978, 151-6. 19th c.

Meols

COOKE, A.H. 'The family of Meols', *B.B.O.A.J.* 33, 1929, 49-50.

Messenger

REED, F.M. 'The early Messengers', *O.F.H.* 5(1), 1989, 21-5. 16-20th c.
See also Cotton

Metcalfe
See Pointer

Miller

MILLER, RALPH. *The Millers of Boddington and Balscote, ca. 1490-1990*. [Oxford]: privately printed, 1991. Boddington, Northamptonshire; Balscott, Oxfordshire.

Mitchell

MITCHELL, J.W. 'Genealogical memoranda relating to the Mitchell family', *M.G.H.* N.S. 3, 1880, 101-2. 18-19th c. extracts from family bible.

More
See Trinder

Morris

LOCK, THERESA A. 'The Morris family remembered', *Record of Witney* 10, 1980, 17-20. 20th c.

Napper

GILLOW, JOSEPH. 'The Napper family register', *Publications of the Catholic Record Society* 1, 1904-5, 133-7. Of Holywell, 16-17th c.

Nash

CRUTCH, PAT. 'The Nash family of Old Woodstock', *O.L.H.* 3(7), 1991, 283-90. 16-17th c.
See also Skillicorne

Norreys

O'CONOR, NORREYS JEPHSON. *Godes peace and the queenes: vicissitudes of a house*. O.U.P., 1934. Norreys family of Weston on the Green.

North
'North', *M.G.H.* 2, 1876, 94-5. Of Buckinghamshire and Oxfordshire; 18th c.

Oilly

POSTLES, DAVID. 'Patronus et advocatus noster: Oseney Abbey and the Oilly family', *Historical research* 60, 1987, 100-102. 12th c.

Page

COOPER, GILLIAN M. 'The Page family of Adderbury', *O.F.H.* 5(5), 1990, 185-9. 19th c., includes will of William Page, 1891.

Passelewe

PREECE, PATRICIA G. 'A family of medieval woodmen', *O.L.H.* 3(1), 1988, 14-17. Passelewe family, 14-15th c.

Perrot

BARNWELL, EDWARD LOWRY. *Perrot notes: or, some account of the various branches of the Perrot family*. J. Russell Smith, 1867. Includes many pedigrees, including that of Perrot of North Leigh.

Perrot *continued*

TOYNBEE, M.R. 'Charles I and the Perrots of Northleigh', *Ox.* **11-12**, 1946-7, 132-46. Includes pedigree, 16-19th c.

'Perrot', *M.G.H.* 3rd series **3**, 1900, 13-17. London and Oxfordshire; 16-17th c.

Phillipps

PHILLIPPS, SIR THOMAS. *Pedigree of Phillips family of Chipping Norton in the county of Oxfordshire.* ed. Ernest Phillips. Croydon: E. Phillipps, 1929. Foldeed pedigree 16-20th c.

Pitcher
See Gill

Plowden

NORSWORTHY, LAURA LUCIE. 'The Plowden interest in Oxfordshire', *Shropshire Archaeological Society transactions* **52**, 1948, 179-90. 16-17th c. landowners of Shiplake; later of Shropshire.

Pointer

CRUMP, J. HAMERTON. 'Pointer pedigree, &c.', *Genealogist* N.S. **3**, 1886, 101-7 & 232-40. 17-18th c., also includes notes on Willoughby, Metcalfe, Williams and Badgers.

Potts

'The Potts family and the Banbury guardian', *C.&Ch.* **10**(6), 1987, 153-7. 19-20th c.

Poure
See Wynslowe

Power

RYLANDS, J. PAUL. 'Grant of arms to Francis Power, of Bletchington, Co.Oxford', *M.G.H.* 4th series **3**, 1910, 241.

See also Danvers

Quatremain

CARTER, WILLIAM F. *The Quatremains of Oxfordshire.* Oxford: O.U.P., 1936. 12-20th c. Includes wills and parish register extracts.

Raynsford

BODDINGTON, REGINALD STEWART. 'Pedigree of Raynsford', *M.G.H.* 3rd series **2**, 1898, 158-64. See also 195-7. Of Oxfordshire and Northamptonshire; 16-19th c.

Rede
See Elkington

Renforth

SCARR, JACK RENFORTH. 'A foray into Chancery', *O.F.H.* **3**(7), 1985, 231-2. Renforth family, 18th c.

Reynolds
See Beesly

Samborne

SANBORN, V.C. 'The Sambornes of England and America', *New England historical and genealogical register* **39**, 1885, 245-55. Of Somerset, Oxfordshire, and Berkshire; includes pedigrees, 11-17th c.

Sherbourne
See Stayt

Skillicorne

WRIGHT, LILIAN. 'An Oxfordshire clerical family: Eynsham and Salford, 1750-1928', *Eynsham record* **6**, 1989, 26-36. Skillicorne, Nash and Bricknell families; includes pedigrees, 18-20th c.

Smythe
See Gill

Spencer-Churchill

MONTGOMERY-MASSINGBERD, HUGH. *Blenheim revisited: the Spencer-Churchills and their palace.* Bodley Head, 1985. Includes pedigree, 17-20th c.

See also Churchill

Stanley

WRIGHT, LILIAN. 'The Stanleys in Eynsham: an outline of the Stanley connections, 1545-1643', *Eynsham record* **2**, 1985, 32-8. Includes pedigree of Stanley, Earls of Derby, 15-17th c., and of Wood, 17th c.

Stayt

TOMBS, JESSICA. 'My family: a short history of a Witney family', *Record of Witney* **2**(4), [1989], 74-9. Includes pedigrees of Stayt and Sherbourne families, 19-20th c.

Stevens

STEVENS, PETER. 'Stevens of Stanton, Horspath and Chinnor', *O.F.H.* **1**(6), 1978, 154-9. 16-20th c., includes list of allied surnames.

Stonor

KINGSFORD, CHARLES LETHBRIDGE, ed. *The Stonor letters and papers, 1290-1483.* 2 vols. Camden 3rd series **29** & **30**. Royal Historical Society, 1919. See also **34**, 1924. Of Oxfordshire, Berkshire and Buckinghamshire; includes pedigree, 13-16th c.

Stonor *continued*

STONOR, ROBERT JULIAN. *Stonor: a Catholic sanctuary in the Chilterns from the fifth century to today.* Newport: R.H. Johns, 1951. Stonor family, includes pedigrees, 12-20th c.

Stretley

MORIARTY, G. ANDREWS. 'The Stretley family of Bucks and Oxon', *Records of Buckinghamshire*, **13**, 1934-40, 379-97. Medieval; includes folded pedigree.

Tagg
See Wrench

Taunton

[TAUNTON, WILLIAM G.] *The Tauntons of Oxford.* Elliot Stock, 1902. Taunton family of Cornwall and Oxfordshire; Grosvenor of Staffordshire; Garrett of Yorkshire and Barbados; includes pedigrees.

Taylor

[TAYLOR, EDMUND DENISON.] *The Taylor family of Riseley, Co.Bedford, St.Neots, Co.Huntingdon, City of Oxford, Buckland Brewer, Co.Devon, Loughborough, Co.Leicester.* Leicester: W. Thornley & Sons, 1933. 18-20th c.

Tracy
See Danvers

Trillowe

TRILLO, HOWARD. 'The Trillowes of Chastleton: a medieval family', *O.F.H.* 3(4 & 5), 1984, 139-42 & 158-61.

Trinder

BROOKS, E.ST.J. 'The Trinders of Holwell, Oxon: a link with Peter Heylyn and Sir Thomas More', *Notes & queries* **152**, 1927, 129-31. 17-18th c.

Tubb

DANNATT, G.H. 'The Tubb family of Bicester and their bank', *O.L.H.* **1**(3), 1981, 21-9. Includes pedigree, 19-20th c.

Tusmore

LEGG, L.G. WICKHAM, ed. *Tusmore papers.* O.R.S. **20**, 1939. Tusmore family letters and papers, 14-19th c. Includes a note on the Gifford family.

Twisleton

FIENNES, D.M. 'The quarterings of the Right Honourable Thomas Twisleton', *C.&Ch.* 7(3), 1977, 89-93.

Umpton
See Danvers, Fiennes and Leigh

Underhill

PAINTIN, H. *Oxford and the Underhill family, 1532-1911.* Oxford: Chronicle Co., 1911. Reprinted from the *Oxford Chronicle* 16 Sept, 1911.

Unton

HOWARD-DRAKE, JACK. 'The Untons', *Wychwoods history* **6**, 1991, 5-18. Unton family, 16th c.

Walgrave
See Danvers

Ward
See Gill

Wentworth

RUTTON, WILLIAM LOFTIE. *Three branches of the family of Wentworth.* [ ]: [the author], 1891. Of Nettlestead, Suffolk, Gosfield, Essex, and Lillingstone Lovell; 15-19th c. Includes pedigrees.

RUTTON, WILLIAM LOFTIE. 'Wentworth of Lillingstone Lovell, Co. Oxford; now Co. Buckingham, *Records of Buckinghamshire*', **6**, 1887, 212-44. Includes pedigrees, 14-18th c.

Weynman

JEWERS, ARTHUR J. 'Exemplification of arms and grant of crest to Richard Weynman, by Thomas Wrythe or Wryothesley, Garter', *M.G.H.* 5th series **1**, 1916, 286-7. 1609.

Whately

CHITTY, E. 'The Whately and Wheatly family of Banbury', *C.&Ch.* **4**, 1968-71, 35-41. Includes pedigree, 16-18th c.

Whorwood

'Confirmation of arms to John Whorwood, Windsor Herald', *M.G.H.* N.S. **4**, 1884, 49-50. 1729-30.

Wickham

L[ONG], C.E. 'Descent of the family of Wickham of Swalcliffe and their kindred to the founder of New College', *Collectanea topographica et genealogica* **2**, 1835, 225-45 & 368-87; **3**, 1836, 178-239 & 345-76. Medieval-19th c., includes pedigree.

MARTIN, C.W. 'Was William of Wykeham of the family of Swalcliffe?', *Topographer & genealogist* **3**, 1858, 49-74.

'Who was William of Wykeham?', *Herald & genealogist* **5**, 1870, 225-35. 14th c.

See also Fiennes

Wickson

BAINBRIDGE, WILLIAM. 'Gran'papa's house',
Eynsham record 3, 1986, 31-40. Includes
pedigree, 18-20th c., showing relationship of
Wickson, Evans, Bainbridge and James.

Wiggins

COUPER, GILLIAN M. 'An Oxfordshire Wiggins
family', *O.F.H.* **4**(4), 1987, 129-31. 18-20th c.

Wilcote

MACNAMARA, F.N. 'The Wilcotes family',
B.B.O.A.J. **3**(4), 1898, 97-107. 14-15th c.

CARTER, W.F. 'The Wilcotes family', *B.B.O.A.J.*
12, 1906-7, 107-13; **13**, 1907-8, 18-21. Reply to
MacNamara.

Wilder

DYER, A. STEPHEN. 'Wilder family of Shiplake,
Oxon., and the American Wilders', *Notes &
queries* **167**, 1934, 148. 17th c.

WILDER, WILLIAM C. *The Wilder family*. Research
Publishing, 1962. Of Ipsden, 16-20th c.
Includes folded pedigree, 18-20th c.

Willcocks

LAMBORN, E.A. GREENING. 'The donor of the pulpit
at North Aston', *O.A.S.* **84**, 1938, 65-6. Includes
folded pedigree of Willcocks, 14-15th c.

Williams

WILLIAMS, BENJAMIN. *Memorials of the family of
Williams of Cote, or Coate in the parish of
Bampton, Oxon.* [ ]: W.A.B. Williams, 1904.
Includes folded pedigrees, 15-20th c.
See also Pointer

Willis

BRADBROOKE, WILLIAM. 'North Hinksey and the
Willis family', *O.A.S.* **81**, 1935, 63-73.
17-18th c.

Willoughby

See Pointer

Wilmot

GREENFIELD, B.W. 'Wilmot and Lee: extract from
the register of the parish church of Adderbury,
Co.Oxford', *M.G.H.* N.S. **1**, 1874, 420-21.
Includes pedigree, 17th c.

Wood

*Pedigrees and memorials of the family of Woodd,
formerly of Shynewood, Salop and Brize
Norton, Oxfordshire; now of Conyngham Hall,
Co.York and Hampstead, Middlesex, extracted
from the records of the College of Arms,
London, 1875.* Mitchell & Hughes, 1875.
15-19th c.
See also Stanley

Woodhull

KING, RUFUS. 'Woodhull entries from the parish
registers of Mollington, Oxford county,
England', *New England historic and
genealogical register* **45**, 1891, 146-9.
See also Elkington

Wrench

BROWN-GRANT, EVELYN. 'The gardeners of
Paradise', *O.F.H.* **3**(7), 1985, 222-5; **3**(9), 1985,
286-9; **4**(1), 1986, 17-22; **4**(2), 1986, 45-52.
Paradise, Oxford was a market garden; this
article traces its occupants—Wrench and Tagg
families, 17-19th c.

Wykeham

See Wickham

Wynslowe

MORIARTY, G. ANDREWS. 'The Wynslowe family',
M.G.H. 5th series **6**, 1926, 110-39.
Worcestershire, Oxfordshire and London;
extracts from deeds, inquisitions post mortem,
wills, etc., 14-15th c., with pedigrees, 14-
16th c., and notes on the Poure family.

7. PARISH REGISTERS AND OTHER RECORDS OF BIRTHS, MARRIAGES AND DEATHS

The importance of parish registers to the genealogist cannot be overstated; they are normally one of the first sources to be consulted. For Oxfordshire, the main guide to their location is:

HARRIS, C.G. *Oxfordshire parish registers and bishops' transcripts.* 4th ed. Oxford: Oxfordshire F.H.S., 1993. This volume includes the registers of that portion of Berkshire transferred to Oxfordshire in 1974. It also lists various marriage indexes, and will be regularly updated in *O.F.H.*. The Banbury portion of an earlier edition was printed as: HARRIS, C.G. 'North Oxfordshire parish registers and modern transcripts', *C.&Ch.* **9**(5), 1984, 148-51. Excludes non-parochial registers and bishops' transcripts but includes Quaker registers of Banbury meeting.

A fuller listing, but now very outdated, is:

STEEL, D.J. *National index of parish registers: a guide to Anlican, Roman Catholic and Nonconformist registers before 1837, together with information on marriage licences, bishops' transcripts and modern copies, 5: South Midlands and Welsh Border, comprising the counties of Gloucestershire, Hertfordshire, Oxfordshire, Shropshire, Warwickshire and Worcestershire.* Society of Genealogists, 1966. Reprinted Phillimore, 1971.

Non-parochial registers at the Public Record Office are also listed in:

'Oxon and North Berks non-parochial registers', *O.F.H.* **2**(3), 1980, 92-4.

No less than eight different indexes to Oxfordshire marriages are discussed in:

'Marriage indexes', *O.F.H.* **1**(9), 1979, 247-50. Some also cover Berkshire, Northamptonshire, Warwickshire and Buckinghamshire.

The most important marriage index was compiled by the Oxfordshire Family History Society, and progress reports were regularly printed in *O.F.H.*. See:

HARRIS, COLIN G. 'The O.F.H.S. marriage index completed', *O.F.H.* **3**(9), 1985, 293-8. Includes list of parishes covered.

HARRIS, COLIN. 'Project report: O.F.H.S. marriage index, 1538-1837', *O.F.H.* **4**(5), 1987, 156-9. Includes a conspectus of microfilm reels filmed by the Mormons, giving reel nos.

That portion of the International Genealogical Index (I.G.I.) covering Oxfordshire is superseded by the O.F.H.S. index. However, it may still prove useful to those without immediate access to the latter. A full listing of registers covered by the I.G.I. is given in:

'Using the I.G.I.', *O.F.H.* **4**(6), 1987, 175-84. Two general works on Oxfordshire parish registers are:

FAULKNER, C. A brief history of parish registers, with remarks on a few of the registers of the North of Oxfordshire', *Transactions of the Archaeological Society of North Oxfordshire, 1853-5*, 101-11. General discussion of contents, of dubious value.

LAMBRICK, GABRIELLE. 'Oxford colleges and some country parishes round Oxford in the early 18th century', *Ox.* **25**, 1960, 109-20. Useful discussion of the impact of the colleges on parochial administration, including the registration of births, marriages and deaths.

Extracts from miscellaneous registers are contained in:

OLDFIELD, W.J. 'Extracts from the parish registers of Oxfordshire', *B.B.O.A.J.* **16**, 1910-11, 57-8, 71-4 & 117-8; **17**, 1911-12, 44-8. Brief extracts from Cassington, Eynsham, Hanborough, Northmoor, Standlake, Stanton Harcourt, and Yarnton.

HANSOM, J.S., ed. 'The Catholic register of the Rev. Monox Hervey alias John Rivett alias John Moxon: Oxfordshire, 1729-30; London, 1730-34; Yorkshire, 1734-47; Montgomeryshire, 1747-52 and London, 1753-56', *Publications of the Catholic Record Society* **14**, 1914.

FOSTER, IRENE. 'Moving around', *O.F.H.* **2**(7), 205-8. Discussion of Middlesex Hospital birth records, with list of entries for Oxfordshire births, 1753-65, and other places outside of London and Middlesex, 1747-51.

Ambrosden

BLAYDES, F.A., ed. 'Extracts from the parish registers of Ambrosden, co.Oxon', *M.G.H.* 2nd series **2**, 1888, 303-4. 17-18th c.

Banbury

GIBSON, J.S.W., ed. *Baptism and burial registers of Banbury, Oxfordshire*. 4 vols. B.H.S. **7, 9, 16, 18 & 22**, 1966-88. Covers 1558-1838. Includes entries from nonconformist registers (including Roman Catholics of Warkworth and Overthorpe) from 1650 for the Quakers, late 18th c. for others. Also includes monumental inscriptions, and collates probate records with burial records. Appendices list probate records pre-dating the register, and those which do not relate to entries in the register. For addenda and corrigenda, see below, section 8B.

GIBSON, J.S.W., ed. *Marriage register of Banbury*. B.H.S. **2-3 & 5**, 1960-63. 1558-1837. This does not include Quaker marriages.

See also Drayton

Bicester Deanery

GOADBY, F.R.L. 'Bicester Deanery jottings', *O.F.H.* **3**(6), 1984, 213-4. Brief notes on parish registers.

Britwell Prior

EDGE, JOHN. 'The Catholic registers of Britwell-Prior, 1765-88 with deaths previously', *Publications of the Catholic Record Society* **13**, 1913, 292-8.

Cassington

OLDFIELD, W.J., ed. 'Marriages at Cassington 1673 to 1837', in PHILLIMORE, W.P.W., AND OLDFIELD, W.J., eds. *O.P.R.M.* **2**. *P.P.R.S.* **160**. Phillimore, 1910, 155-66.

Chipping Norton

Chipping-Norton register. Middlehill: [Typis Medio Montanis], 1830. 16-17th c.

WELLSTOOD, F.C., AND LITTLEDALE, G.A., eds. 'Marriages at Chipping Norton, 1560 to 1837', in PHILLIMORE, W.P.W., ed. *O.P.R.M.* **1**. *P.P.R.S.* **104**. Phillimore, 1909, 1-97.

MANN, RALPH. 'Chipping Norton Baptists: register of births', *O.F.H.* **3**(6), 1984, 190-91. General discussion noting some surnames.

Crowell

SPENCER, MISS, AND DAVIS, F.N., eds. 'Marriages at Crowell, 1602 to 1836', in PHILLIMORE, W.P.W., & MARRIOTT, F.R., eds. *O.P.R.M.* **1**. *P.P.R.S.* **104**. Phillimore, 1909, 151-6.

Culham

BRADBROOKE, WILLIAM. 'Culham, Co.Oxon: the parish register', *O.A.S.* **79**, 1933, 22-8. Brief notes.

Drayton

G[IBSON], J.S.W. 'Banbury marriages at Drayton in 1790', *C.&Ch.* **5**, 1971-4, 78. Contracted whilst Banbury church was being demolished and rebuilt.

Ducklington

MACRAY, W.D. *An index to the registers of baptisms, marriages and burials in the parish of Ducklington*. Oxford: Parker & Co., 1880. Published as *Transactions of the North Oxfordshire Archaeological Society*, 1880.

Emmington

CHINNOR HISTORICAL AND ARCHAEOLOGICAL SOCIETY. *St.Nicholas Church, Emmington: an analysis of church registers*. Occasional paper **2**. Chinnor: Chinnor Historical & Archaeological Society, 1978. Includes some extracts, but primarily an analysis.

Eynsham

OLDFIELD, W.J., ed. 'Marriages at Eynsham, 1665 to 1837', in PHILLIMORE, W.P.W., AND OLDFIELD, W.J., eds. *O.P.R.M.* **2**. *P.P.R.S.* **160**. Phillimore, 1910, 1-30.

Finmere

ROBINSON, CHARLES J. 'Church notes from Finmere, Co.Oxon', *Genealogist* N.S. **2**, 1885, 48-9 & 103-6. Includes extracts from the parish register, monumental inscriptions, list of rectors, and pedigree of Hogan, 17-18th c.

Glympton

BARNETT, HERBERT. *Glympton: the history of an Oxfordshire manor*. O.R.S. **5**, 1923. The parish register, 1567-1657 and 1667-1812 occupies almost 50% of this volume. Also included are monumental inscriptions, a list of rectors, a descent of the manor, pedigree of Cupper, 16-17th c., Wheate, 17-19th c., Barnett, 18-20th c., etc., etc.

Hanborough

OLDFIELD, W.J., ed. 'Marriages at Hanborough, 1560 to 1837', in PHILLIMORE, W.P.W., AND OLDFIELD, W.J., eds. *O.P.R.M.* **2**. *P.P.R.S.* **160**. Phillimore, 1910, 89-121.

Kiddington

BALL, HENRY HOUSTON. 'The Catholic registers of the domestic chapel of the Browne-Mostyn family at Kiddington, 1788-1840', *Publications of the Catholic Record Society* **17**, 1915, 455-78.

Kidlington

MARTIN, R.C. *Kidlington parish registers, 1574-1837*. Kidlington: Kidlington & District Historical Society, 1981. For Kidlington marriages, 1574-1754, see section 5 above.

Launton

TUCKER, PAT. 'Launton', *O.F.H.* 2(6), 1981, 167-9. Discusses index of Launton surnames, based initially on the parish register, and lists common surnames, 1716-1881.

Littlemore

COOMBS, D.W. 'Littlemore inhabitants', *O.F.H.* 2(2), 1980, 51-2. Discusses transcription of the register.

Merton

MASSEY, E.R. 'An account of the parish registers of Merton and of the recovery of a missing portion', *O.A.S.* 44, 1902, 23-6. Brief note.

Northmoor

OLDFIELD, W.J., ed. 'Marriages at Northmoor, 1654 to 1837', in PHILLIMORE, W.P.W., AND OLDFIELD, W.J., eds. *O.P.R.M.* 2. *P.P.R.S.* 160. Phillimore, 1910, 123-35.

Overthorpe

See Banbury

Oxford

HARRIS, COLIN G. 'Marriages in Oxford before 1754', *O.F.H.* 2(9), 1982, 278-85. General discussion with some extracts, and a list of registers.

GIBSON, J.S.W. *Marriages at Oxford, 1813-1837: an alphabetical digest*. Oxford: Oxfordshire Local History Society, 1979. From the registers of 14 city parishes.

GIBSON, J.S.W. 'Roman Catholic baptisms in Oxford, 1835-1837', *O.F.H.* 2(7), 1982, 223-4. This continues the Waterperry register, see below.

'The register booke of Christ Church in Oxford of all that have been christened, maried, and buried since ... 1633', *M.G.H.* 2nd series 1, 1886, 143-6 & 288-95; 2, 1888, 198-200, 215-8, 236-7, 251-4 & 268-71. Burials 1639-1882; baptisms 1633-1864; marriages, 1642-1884.

SCARR, JACK. 'Registers of St.Mary Magdalen, Oxford', *O.F.H.* 4(8), 1988, 254-6; 5(2), 1989, 58-60, and 5(5), 1990, 184-5. See also 5(3), 1989, 105-6, and 5(5), 1990, 207-8. General discussion, noting many names.

Pyrton

SALTER, H.E., ed. 'Marriages at Pyrton, 1563 to 1812', in PHILLIMORE, W.P.W., AND MARRIOTT, F.R., eds. *O.P.R.M.* 1. *P.P.R.S.* 104. Phillimore, 1909, 129-50.

Shiplake

YOUNG, ELIZABETH. 'Shiplake marriages, 1644-1653', *O.F.H.* 2(2), 1980, 34. General discussion.

Shipton under Wychwood

HOWARD-DRAKE, JACK. 'Shipton-under-Wychwood registers', *O.F.H.* 3(2), 1982, 61-2. Brief note.

Standlake

'Marriages at Standlake, 1559 to 1837', in PHILLIMORE, W.P.W., AND OLDFIELD, W.J., eds. *O.P.R.M.* 2. *P.P.R.S.* 160. Phillimore, 1910, 53-88.

Stanton Harcourt

OLDFIELD, W.J., ed. 'Marriages at Stanton Harcourt, 1570 to 1837', in PHILLIMORE, W.P.W., AND OLDFIELD, W.J., eds. *O.P.R.M.* 2. *P.P.R.S.* 160. Phillimore, 1910, 31-52.

Summertown

SCARR, JACK RENFORTH. 'The parish registers of Summertown', *O.F.H.* 4(3), 94-6. General discussion; many names.

Swinbrook

GIBSON, J.S.W., ed. 'Registers of Swinbrook, near Burford, in Oxfordshire', *Genealogists quarterly* 25(2), 1958, 51-63. 1685-1837. Marriages only.

Warkworth

See Banbury

Waterperry

HANSOM, JOSEPH STANISLAUS. 'Catholic register of the domestic chapel at Waterperry manor house, Oxon, and St.Clements church, Oxford, 1701?-1834?', *Publications of the Catholic Record Society* 7, 1909, 388-434. For continuation, see Oxford.

Witney

'Witney parish registers, 1551-1837', *Record of Witney* 4, 1978, 5-7. Detailed listing of many volumes; no extracts.

Witney Deanery

GOADBY, F.R.L. 'Jottings from parish registers, Witney Deanery', *O.F.H.* 3(2), 1983, 42-7. Brief notes made during the O.F.H.S. transcription project.

Wolvercote

SCARR, J.R. 'Wolvercote registers', *O.F.H.* 1(8), 1979, 212-4. General discussion, listing some common surnames.

SCARR, J.R. 'Wolvercote since 1840', *O.F.H.* 2(5), 1981, 147-9. Notes on the transcription of the parish register, listing all surnames with over 30 entries.

Bradfield, Berks, and Wolvercote, Oxon: notes from the parish registers, 16th & 17th cent. Oxford: Bridge & Co., 1888. Extracts.

Woodstock

WOODWARD, ELIZABETH. 'First names in Woodstock baptismal registers', *O.F.H.* 4(2), 1986, 60-61.

Woodstock Deanery

GOADBY, F.R.L. 'More parish jottings: Woodstock Deanery', *O.F.H.* 3(4), 1984, 135-8. Notes on parish registers.

Wootton

PHILLIMORE, W.P.W., AND MARRIOTT, F.R., eds. 'Marriages at Wootton, 1564 to 1837', in PHILLIMORE, W.P.W., ed. *O.P.R.M.* 1. *P.P.R.S.* 104. Phillimore, 1909, 99-128.

Yarnton

OLDFIELD, W.J., ed. 'Marriages at Yarnton, 1569 to 1837', in PHILLIMORE, W.P.W., AND OLDFIELD, W.J., eds. *O.P.R.M.* 2. *P.P.R.S.* 160. Phillimore, 1910, 137-53.

8. PROBATE RECORDS

A. GENERAL

Probate records—wills, inventories, administration bonds, etc.—are invaluable sources of genealogical information. Most wills list all living children; other relatives are often mentioned, as are places with which the testator has been associated. A useful, but now out of date, guide to their whereabouts is provided by:

GIBSON, J.S.W. 'Pre-1858 probate records of Oxfordshire and Berkshire testators', *O.F.H.* 1(9), 1979, 241-5.

The majority of pre-1858 Oxfordshire wills were proved in either the Consistory Court of the Bishop of Oxford, or in the court of the Archdeacon of Oxford. For indexes to these wills, see:

CHEYNE, ERNEST. *Probate records of the courts of the bishop and archdeacon of Oxford, 1516-1732.* ed. D.M. Barratt. 2 vols. Index library **93-4**. British Record Society, 1981-5.

WOOD, LESLIE W. 'In the name of God, Amen', *O.F.H.* 2(2), 1980, 40-48. General discussion of Oxfordshire wills, 1733-1800, and the compilation of an index.

WOOD, LESLIE W. 'Oxfordshire probates 1733-1800: the next step', *O.F.H.* 2(7), 1982, 225-6. Discussion of place-name and occupational indexes then in the Bodleian Library, now in the Oxfordshire Archives.

A number of other courts also exercised probate jurisdiction in Oxfordshire; indexes or abstracts of wills from a number of them have been published:

GIBSON, J.S.W. *Index to wills proved in the peculiar court of Banbury, 1542-1858.* B.H.S. **1**, 1959. Also published in *O.R.S.* **40**, 1959, 1-76. The court's jurisdiction included the Oxfordshire parishes of Horley, Hornton, Banbury (partly in Northamptonshire) and Cropredy (partly in Warwickshire); Kings Sutton, Northamptonshire, was also covered. This volume also includes wills proved in the manorial court of Sibford, in the parish of Swalcliffe. A much fuller listing of the latter, mainly 1724-59, is to be found in: HOAD, JOYCE. 'Wills from the manorial court of Sibford Gower', *O.F.H.* 2(8), 1982, 267-9.

ELLIS, WILLIAM PATTERSON. *Liber albus Civitatis Oxoniensis: abstract of the wills, deeds, and enrolments contained in the White Book of the City of Oxford.* Oxford: Oxford Chronicle Co., 1909. Medieval.

GRIFFITHS, JOHN. *An index of wills proved in the Court of the Chancellor of the University of Oxford, and to such of the records and other instruments and papers of that ccourt as relate to matters or causes testamentary.* Oxford: University Press, 1862.

Many Oxfordshire wills were proved in the Prerogative Court of Canterbury—the principal probate court. For them, reference should be made to the indexes and abstracts listed in *English genealogy: an introductory bibliography* section 11. A number of local indexes are also available:

WEAVER, J.R.H., AND BEARDWOOD, A., eds. *Some Oxfordshire wills proved in the Prerogative Court of Canterbury, 1393-1510.* O.R.S. **58**, 1958.

'Oxfordshire testators in the P.C.C. wills index, 1750-1800', *O.F.H.* **1**(6), 1978, 166-8 (A-Ce); **3**(6), 1984, 192-5, (C-G); **4**(9), 1988, 286-90 (H-M); **6**(3), 1992 (N-S). Index; to be continued.

GIBSON, J.S.W. 'Oxfordshire probate inventories in the records of the Prerogative Court of Canterbury', *O.L.H.* **1**(2), 1981, 24-30; **1**(3), 1981, 16-20. Includes list, 1660-early 18th c.

GIBSON, J.S.W. 'Berkshire and Oxfordshire wills and admons in the Prerogative Court of Canterbury for the year 1801', *O.F.H.* **1**(7), 1979, 215-20. Index for a single year.

VANN, RICHARD T. 'Banbury wills in the Prerogative Court of Canterbury 1701-1723', *C.&Ch.* **5**, 1971-4, 18-20. List.

Wills found in collections of family papers are listed in:

GRANT, J.S. 'Stray wills and admons in the Oxon R.O.', *O.F.H.* **2**(3 & 4), 1980-81, 78-86 & 107-18.

For a discussion of an index to wills in Ploughley Hundred, see:

SMITH, DONNETTE STRINGHAM. 'Ploughley Hundred probate records', *O.F.H.* **1**(3), 1977, 68-9.

B. PUBLISHED ABSTRACTS

A number of editors have brought together and published collections of wills and inventories. These include:

HAVINDEN, M.A., ed. *Household and farm inventories in Oxfordshire, 1550-1590.* O.R.S. **44**, 1965. Also published in the Historical Manuscripts Commission joint publications series **10**.

GIBSON, STRICKLAND. *Abstracts from the wills and testamentary documents of binders, printers and stationers of Oxford, from 1493 to 1638.* Bibliographical Society, 1907. Proved in the Chancellor's Court.

Banbury

BRINKWORTH, E.R.C., AND GIBSON, J.S.W., eds. *Banbury wills and inventories.* B.H.S. **13-14**, 1976-85. Pt.1 1591-1620. Pt.2. 1621-1650. Will abstracts etc. for 403 testators from the Banbury Peculiar Court. Appendices list Banbury testators, 1571-90; and Banbury wills proved in the Prerogative Court of Canterbury, 1591-1650. A list of wills 1510-70 is printed with the register (above, section 7); see also: GIBSON, J.S.W. 'Probate records information in Banbury burial registers 1558-1653: addenda and corrigenda', *C.&Ch.* **11**(1), 1988, 25-8.

TRINDER, BARRIE, AND GIBSON, JEREMY. 'Living in Banbury, 1660-1730: a foretaste', *C.&Ch.* **10**(9), 225-37. See also **11**(1), 1988, 28. Mainly notes on probate inventories, with biographical details, and list of P.C.C. inventories 1663-1747.

Emmington

CHINNOR HISTORICAL AND ARCHAEOLOGICAL SOCIETY. *Emmington wills and inventories (held in the Bodleian Library) 1548-1721.* Monograph 1. Looseleaf. Chinnor: Chinnor Historical and Archaeological Society, [1979?]

CHINNOR HISTORICAL AND ARCHAEOLOGICAL SOCIETY. *Emmington 1697.* Occasional paper **3**. Chinnor: the Society, 1979. Includes 10 further wills and inventories, with hearth tax returns, 1662 to 1665.

Water Eaton

OFFORD, V.E., ed. *The probate documents of Water Eaton, Oxfordshire, 1592-1730.* Kidlington: Kidlington and District Historical Society, 1986.

C. INDIVIDUAL WILLS, etc.

Benbow

KENNEDY, M.J.O. 'A Banbury seafarer', *C.&Ch.* **4**, 1968-71, 41-3. Based on the will of William Benbow, 1692.

Brasbridge

B[RINKWORTH], E.R.C. 'The inventory of Thomas Brasbridge, 1594', *C.&Ch.* **3**(5), 1966, 71-4.

Calcott

COLTMAN, SUE. 'A Hook Norton family: the Calcotts', *C.&Ch.* **9**(1), 1982, 7-13. Includes will and inventory of Alexander Calcott, 1682.

Probate Records continued

Carter
RICHARDS, PAMELA. 'Where there's a will, there's a story', *Eynsham record* **2**, 1985, 11-15. Discussion of the will of Ann Carter, 1628.

Coren
See King

English
COSTIN, W.C. 'The inventory of John English, B.C.L., fellow of St.Johns College', *Ox.* **11**, 1946-7, 102-31. 1613.

Fermor
SHIRLEY, EVELYN PHILIP. 'Extracts from the Fermor accounts, A.D. 1580', *Archaeological journal* **8**, 1851, 179-86. Extract from the will of Thomas Fermor of Somerton, with his executor's accounts.

Fiennes
SLADE, HARRY GORDON. 'Inventories of Broughton Castle in 1662 and 1731 with commentary', *C.&Ch.* **8**(6), 1981, 155-71. Probate inventories of William Fiennes, Lord Saye and Sele, 1662, and of Fiennes Twisleton, 1731. Includes pedigrees, 16-17th c., showing relationship to Lucy and Gardner.
'Nathaniel Fiennes (1608-1669)', *C.&Ch.* **9**(5), 1984, 143-7. Will.
'Inventory of goods of Nathaniel Fiennes, died 1669', *C.&Ch.* **9**(2), 1983, 38-48.

Fisher
HIGHFIELD, J.R.L. 'Alexander Fisher, Sir Christopher Wren, and Merton College chapel', *Ox.* **25**, 1960, 70-82. Includes Fisher's probate account, c.1672, giving many names of workmen in the chapel.

Holloway
BODDINGTON, REGINALD STEWART. 'Unpublished wills and administrations', *M.G.H.* 2nd series **5**, 1894, 50-52. Includes wills of the Holloway family of London and Oxfordshire, 17-18th c.

Huckvale
DUNLOP, J. RENTON. 'Huckvale', *M.G.H.* 5th series **4**, 1920-22, 258-9. Wills, 16th c.

Hyatt
JOURDAN, SUE. 'The probate inventory of William Hyatt, 1587', *Wychwoods history* **1**, 1985, 60-64.

King
PEARCE, S. SPENCER. 'Three sixteenth century clerical wills', *O.A.S.* **1923**, 323-33. Robert King, Bishop of Oxford, 1557; Hugh Coren, Archbishop of Dublin, 1564; Walter Wright, Archdeacon of Oxford, 1561.

Paty
EYNSHAM PRIMARY SCHOOL RESEARCH GROUP. 'The will of John Paty, boatman, died 1674', *Eynsham record* **6**, 1989, 18-23.

Reeve
REEVE, R.W. REed. 'Will of John Reeve of Gt.Milton, Co.Oxford', *East Anglian miscellany*, 1917, 77-8.

St.John
SALTER, H., ed. 'An Oxfordshire will of 1230-1231', *English Historical Review* **20**, 1905, 291-2. John of St.John.

Simmons
See Whistler

Southam
'Thomas Southam, Archdeacon of Berks and Oxon', *B.B.O.A.J.* **6**(1), 1990, 18-22. Will, 1403/4.

Twisleton
See Fiennes

Webb
GIBSON, J.S.W. 'A disputed inheritance', *C.&Ch.* **6**, 1974-6, 83-6. Discusses will of John Webb, 1641, and his bequest to Ann Vivers nee Hawtyn, the subject of an ecclesiastical court case.

Whistler
WILLIAMS, ETHEL CARLETON. 'Notes on Whistler and Simmons charities at Goring', *Berkshire archaeological journal* **41**, 1937, 58-67. Includes wills of Lettice Simmons, 1700, and Ellinor Whistler, 1630, and list of recipients of the Whistler charity 1639.

Williams
Some account of Lord Williams of Thame, founder of the grammar school and the alms-houses at Thame, together with the copy of his will and copies of very valuable English and Latin documents relating to the above charity. Thame: C. Ellis, 1873. Will dated 1559.

Wright
See King

9. MONUMENTAL INSCRIPTIONS

A. *GENERAL*

Monumental inscriptions are an important source of genealogical information. Many have been transcibed by the Oxfordshire Family History Society; transcripts (including some for that part of Berkshire now in Oxfordshire) are listed in:

YOUNG, LIZ. 'Project: monumental inscriptions', *O.F.H.* 4(7), 1988, 232-4. Most transcripts are now available on microfiche.

Many inscriptions are included in:

DAVIS, F.N., ed. *Parochial collections made by Anthony A. Wood and Richard Rawlinson.* O.R.S. 2, 4, & 11, 1920-29. Also includes other material.

A general work on Oxfordshire epitaphs is:

UTECHIN, PATRICIA. *Epitaphs from Oxfordshire.* Oxford: Robert Dugdale, 1980.

In the early 19th century, Sir Thomas Phillipps collected many Oxfordshire inscriptions, and published them in:

PHILLIPPS, T. *Parochial collections for the County of Oxford.* [Middle Hill]: Typis Medio Montanis], 1825. Alphabetical, but only completed to Eynsham. Mainly inscriptions.

For brasses, see:

The Oxford portfolio of monumental brasses. 5 pts. Oxford: Oxford University Brass-Rubbing Society, 1898-1901. Includes many Oxfordshire brasses, as well as some from other counties.

The Oxford journal of monumental brasses, being the journal of the Oxford University Brass-Rubbing Society. 2 vols. Oxford: the Society, 1897-1912.

Notes on brass-rubbing, with a list of some brasses in the Oxford region and a summary of the remaining figure brasses in the British Isles. 7th ed. Oxford: Ashmolean Museum, 1976.

BERTRAM, JEROME. 'A Regency collection of brass rubbings', *Monumental Brass Society transactions* 12, 1975, 90-100. Collected by Henry Hinton and James Hunt, 18-19th c., in Oxfordshire and Berkshire. Includes a gazetteer.

STEPHENSON, MILL. 'A list of palimpsest brasses: Oxfordshire', *Monumental Brass Society transactions* 4(7), 1903, 251-62.

See also:

RUCK, G.A.E. 'Additions to the list from Bedfordshire, Northamptonshire, Oxfordshire, Rutland and Shropshire', *Transactions of the Monumental Brass Society* 9(1), 1952, 27-38.

Heraldic works include:

COPE, HAUTENVILLE. 'Selections from notes on the heraldry in Oxfordshire churches', *O.A.S.* 74, 1929, 233-52.

WERE, F. 'Heraldic notes taken during the Oxford meeting', *Bristol and Gloucestershire Archaeological Society transactions* 34, 1911, 120-5.

LAMBORN, E.A. GREENING. *The armorial glass of the Oxford Diocese, 1250-1850.* O.U.P. for Berkshire Archaeological Society, 1949. Berkshire, Buckinghamshire and Oxfordshire.

LAMBORN, E.A. GREENING. 'The armorial glass of the Oxford Diocese', *Berkshire Archaeological journal* 46, 1942, 45-53 & 88-96; 47, 1943, 24-45.

LAMBORN, E.A. GREENING. 'The armorial fonts of the Oxford Diocese', *Berkshire Archaeological journal* 45, 1941, 106-19; & 46, 1942, 32-4.

SUMMERS, PETER, ed. *Hatchments in Britain, 4: Bedfordshire, Berkshire, Buckinghamshire, Oxfordshire and Wiltshire.* Phillimore, 1983.

COLE, A.C. 'Tudor impalements and cadency marks illustrated from stained glass formerly at Sarsden House, Oxfordshire', *Notes & queries* 196, 1951, 442-5 & 463-8. Includes many references to Fettiplace family.

B. *BY PLACE*

Adderbury

FEARSON, W.W. 'A catalogue of the brasses in Adderbury church, Oxfordshire', *O.J.M.B.* 1(2), 1897, 79-80.

Banbury

BEESLEY, ALFRed. *The history of Banbury including historical and antiquarian notices of the neighbourhood.* Nichols & Son, 1841. Includes monumental inscriptions and many extracts from genealogical sources.

Notes relating to the town and church of Banbury, now first printed from the mss. collections of Dr. Rawlinson preserved in the Bodleian Library, Oxford. Banbury: North Oxfordshire Archaeological Society, 1861. Issued with the Society's *Report*, 1860-61. Mainly monumental inscriptions.

G[IBSON], J.S.W. 'Monuments and their inscriptions in Saint Mary's churchyard, Banbury', *C.&Ch.* 7(5), 1978, 157-8. General discussion. See *B.H.S.* 18 (listed above, section 7) for the inscriptions themselves.

Benson

FIELD, J.E. 'Monumental brasses in Benson church, Oxon', *O.J.M.B.* 1(5), 1898, 208-10.

Bicester

'Bicester: churchyard M.I's reprinted from Dunkin's *History of Bicester*', *O.F.H.* **1**(1), 1977, 6.

'Church notes from Burcester, Oxfordshire', *Topographer* **2**, 1790, 305-12.

Broughton

'Miscellaneous epitaphs in the church of Broughton by Banbury', *Topographer* **2**, 1790, 110-11.

Burford

'Some account of Burford in Oxfordshire, with church notes from a ms in the Brit. Mus.', *Topographer* **2**, 1790, 348-53.

Cassington

See Oxford

Chalgrove

See Stadhampton

Chickendon

See South Stoke

Chipping Norton

MANNING, P. 'Notes on the monumental brasses in Chipping Norton church', *O.J.M.B.* **1**(1), 1897, 3-10.

Cropredy

KEEGAN, PAMELA. 'Cropredy', *O.F.H.* **1**(4), 1978, 90-92. Discusses the results of a project to transcribe monumental inscriptions, and includes a list of families for whom the author has information culled from various sources.

Emmington

CHINNOR HISTORICAL AND ARCHAEOLOGICAL SOCIETY. *St.Nicholas church, Emmington: churchyard survey.* Occasional paper **1**. Chinnor: Chinnor Historical and Archaeological Society, 1978. Includes inscriptions.

Ewelme

BARKER, W.R. 'A catalogue of the brasses in Ewelme church', *O.J.M.B.* **1**(1), 1897, 11-22.

Eynsham

RICHARDS, DONALD. 'Grave stones in the chancel of St.Leonards', *Eynsham record* **5**, 1988, 35-8. Eynsham.

Great Haseley

DE WATTEVILLE, H.G. 'Monumental brasses in the church of Great Haseley, Oxon', *O.J.M.B.* **1**(4), 1898, 170-75.

Great Tew

See Thame

Headington

EMDEN, A.B. 'Tombstones and tiles at St.Andrews church, Headington', *Ox.* **26**/7, 1961/2, 339-40. Includes some inscriptions.

Henley

MANNING, PERCY. 'Monumental brasses in the Deanery of Henley-on-Thames, Oxon', *O.J.M.B.* **1**, 1898, 237-54 & 286-306.

Holton

See Thame

Hook Norton

TILLER, KATE. 'Village dissenters: Hook Norton Baptist Chapel and its chapelyard', *C.&Ch.* **9**(1), 1982, 27-31, & **9**(3), 1983, 73. Includes a discussion of memorials.

Ipsden

See South Stoke

Kidlington

St.Mary's, Kidlington, churchyard inscriptions. Kidlington: Kidlington & District Historical Society, 1981.
See also Oxford

Mapledurham

'Mapledurham church, Oxfordshire', *Topographer* **1**, 1889, 410-3.

Middleton Stoney

STEWART, FRAN. 'Life and death in a country churchyard: Middleton Stoney', *O.F.H.* **1**(6), 1978, 145-53. Reprinted from *Local historian* **13**(3), 1978. General discussion, analysing the information found on memorials.

Milton

CHAPMAN, JACK. 'The Milton graveyard survey', *Wychwoods history* **1**, 1985, 34-9. General discussion of memorials, but few names.

CHAPMAN, JACK. 'A survey of the Baptist burial ground, Milton under Wychwood', *Wychwoods history* **2**, 1986, 29-31. General discussion.

North Leigh

'Church notes, &c from North Leigh, Oxfordshire', *Topographer* **3**, 1790, 128-30.

Monumental Inscriptions continued

North Stoke
See South Stoke

Oxford
ROYAL COMMISSION ON HISTORICAL MONUMENTS ENGLAND. *An inventory of the historical monuments in the City of Oxford.* H.M.S.O., 1939. Includes notes on many monumental inscriptions, with an 'Armorial of heraldry before 1550'.

BERTRAM, JEROME. 'The lost brasses of Oxford', *Monumental Brass Society transactions* 11, 1973, 219-52 & 321-79.

SYMONDS, RICHARD. 'Oxford church notes, 1643-4', ed. Rose Graham. *O.H.S.* 47, 1905, 99-134. Includes some heraldry and inscriptions.

BLAKISTON, C.H. 'Monumental brasses and matrices in the Cathedral church of Christ in Oxford', *O.J.M.B.* 1(6), 1899, 268-86.

BLOXHAM, M.H. 'Sepulchral monuments in Oxford Cathedral', *Archaeological journal* 9, 1852, 150-7. General discussion.

RICHARDSON, W.H. 'Inscriptions on stones on the floor of the cloisters of the Cathedral, Oxford', *Genealogist* 4, 1880, 125-6.

ROWSE, A.L. 'Holywell Cemetery: Victorian Oxford', *Contemporary review* 219, 1971, 93-9. General discussion.

MANNING, PERCY. 'Monumental brasses in the churches of St.Aldate and St.Peter-le-Bailey, Oxford', *O.J.M.B.* 1(3), 1897, 103-9.

MANNING, PERCY. 'Monumental brasses in the churches of St.Mary Magdalene, Oxford, and Cassington, Kidlington, Woodstock and Yarnton, Oxon', *O.J.M.B.* 1(5), 1898, 176-90.

JACKSON, T.G. *The church of St.Mary the Virgin, Oxford.* Oxford: Clarendon Press, 1897. Includes monumental inscriptions.

HUNT, A.A. 'Monumental brasses in St.Michael's church and Exeter College chapel, Oxford', *O.J.M.B.* 2(2), 1900, 90-96.

HUNT, A.A. 'Monumental brasses in the churches of St.Peter-in-the-East and St.Cross, Holywell', *O.J.M.B.* 1(4), 1898, 190-200.

Published monumental inscriptions from Oxford colleges will be listed in a forthcoming bibliography dealing solely with the Universities.

Rotherfield Greys
LAMBORN, E.A. GREENING. 'The armorial glass in the Knollys chapel, Rotherfield Greys', *O.A.S.* 84, 1938, 62-4. 17th c.

Shiplake
YOUNG, ELIZABETH. 'Shiplake', *O.F.H.* 1(4), 1978, 97-9. Describes a project to record monumental inscriptions, and includes a list of families for whom the author has further information culled from various sources.

Somerton
'Church notes, &c., of Somerton, in Oxfordshire', *Topographer* 3, 1790, 89-95.

South Stoke
KEYSER, CHARLES E. 'Notes on the churches of South Stoke, North Stoke, Ipsden and Chickendon', *Journal of the British Archaeological Association* N.S. 24, 1918, 1-32. Includes inscriptions.

Stadhampton
DE WATTEVILLE, H.G. 'A catalogue of the brasses in the churches of Stadhampton, Chalgrove and Waterperry, Oxon', *O.J.M.B.* 1(3), 1897, 110-20.

Stanton St.John
MANNING, PERCY. 'Palimpsest brasses from Quarrendon, Bucks., and Stanton St.John, Oxon', *O.J.M.B.* 2(3), 1912, 153-6.

Swinbrook
'Monuments, brasses, etc., at S.Mary's, Swinbrook', *O.A.S.* 47, 1904, 10-16.

Tackley
LAMBORN, E.A. GREENING. 'Arms on the nave roof, Tackley', *O.A.S.* 84, 1938, 57-9.

Thame
BARKER, W.R. 'Monumental brasses in the churches of Thame, Holton, and Great Tew, Oxon., with biographical and genealogical notes', *O.J.M.B.* 1(4), 1898, 137-69. Includes pedigree of Baldington, 16-17th c.

LEE, FREDERICK G. *The history, description and antiquities of the prebendal church of the Blessed Virgin Mary of Thame ...* Mitchell & Hughes, 1853. Includes many pedigrees, monumental inscriptions, extracts form the parish registers, 17-18th c., etc.

Waterperry
'Church notes &c. from Waterperry, in Oxfordshire', *Topographer* 2, 1790, 362-5.
See also Stadhampton

Witney
'Church notes &c. at Whitney', *Topographer* 4, 1791, 155-60.

Woodstock
See Oxford

Yarnton
GOUGH, H. *Heraldic notices of Yarnton church, Oxfordshire*. Oxford: L. Shrimpton, 1844.
See also Oxford

C. *BY FAMILY*
Atkinson
SANDERSON, H. K. ST. J. 'Richard Atkinson, 1574: St Peter in the East, Oxford', *Transactions of the Monumental Brass Society* 2, 1892-6, 143-5.
Byschoppesdon
'Oxfordshire: Broughton', *Transactions of the Cambridge University Association of Brass Collectors* 6, 1888, 44. Brasses of Byschoppesdon, undated, and Fiennes, 1666.

Chaucer
LAMBORN, E.A. GREENING. 'The arms on the Chaucer tomb at Ewelme', *Ox.* 5, 1940, 78-93. Includes pedigree, 14-15th c.

Cornwall
PRICE, E.R. 'Two effigies in the churches of Asthall and Cogges in Oxfordshire', *Ox.* 3, 1938, 103-10. Cornwall and Grey families; includes medieval pedigrees.

Curson
TODD, JOHN. 'The palimpsest brass in Waterperry church', *Transactions of the Monumental Brass Society* 8(6), 1949, 246-50. To Walter Curson, 1527.

Danvers
SPOKES, P.S. 'The heraldry of the chimneypiece in Queen Anne's room, Broughton Castle', *C.&Ch.* 4, 1968-71, 13-14. Danvers and Fiennes families, 16th c.

Drayton
SMITH, J. CHALLENOR. 'Brass of Sir John Drayton, Dorchester, Oxon', *O.J.M.B.* 2(1), 1900, 47-8.

Du Plessis
HEMP, W.J. 'A re-used memorial at Hook Norton', *Transactions of the Monumental Brass Society* 8, 1949, 205-6. To Isabel Du Plessis, 13th c.

Dyve
See Howard

Fermoure
EVANS, H.F.O. 'The palimpsest brass to William Fermoure and wife at Somerton', *Transactions of the Monumental Brass Society* 9(3), 1954, 98-104. 1552.

Fettiplace
DUNLOP, J. RENTON. 'Brasses commemorative of the Fettiplace family', *Transactions of the Monumental Brass Society* 6(2), 1911, 95-119. In Berkshire, Buckinghamshire, Oxfordshire and Sussex.

Fiennes
See Byschoppesdon and Danvers

Goodwin
'Monumental inscriptions of the Goodwin family in Horley church and churchyard', *M.G.H.* 4th series 2, 1908, 39.

Grey
See Cornwall

Hamsterley
TORR, V.J.B. 'The Oddington shroud brass and its lost fellows', *Transactions of the Monumental Brass Society* 7, 1934-42, 225-35. Brass of Ralph Hamsterley, 1518.

Howard
COPE, E.E. 'Heraldry: two Oxfordshire discoveries', *Notes & queries* 157, 1929, 59-60. Howard, Dyve and Mantell families.

Lovel
LAMBORN, E.A. GREENING. 'The Lovel tomb at Minster', *O.A.S.* 83, 1937, 13-20. Minster Lovell; includes medieval pedigree.
LAMBORN, E.A. GREENING. 'The Lovel tomb at Minster', *Notes & queries* 192, 1947, 49-50. Minster Lovell.

Mantell
See Howard

Martin
WRIGHT, LILIAN. 'The Martin memorial in St.Leonards, Eynsham: a link with Jane Austen', *Eynsham record* 8, 1991, 41. Includes pedigree showing relationship of Knight and Austen, 17-18th c.

Parkers
EVANS, H.F. 'Brasses to canons of Windsor', *Transactions of the Monumental Brass Society* 7(6), 1939, 259-60. To Roger Parkers at North Stoke, 1363, and Arthur Cole at Magdalen College, Oxford, 1558.

Reade
'The Reade chapel', *Wychwoods history* 5, 1989, 48-9. At Shipton; includes list of Reade family burials, 18-19th c.

Rede

STEPHENSON, MILL. 'A palimpsest brass at Checkendon', *Transactions of the Monumental Brass Society* 3(1), 1897, 87-8. Edmund Rede, 1435.

Smyh

EVANS, H.F. OWEN. 'The lade who died on the 30th February', *Transactions of the Monumental Brass Society* 9, 1954, 362-3. Jane, wife of George Smyh, of Adderbury, 1508.

Stapleton

FIELD, J.E. 'The Stapleton brass at Ipsden', *B.B.O.A.J.* 14, 1909, 107-10. Medieval.

Taylor

RENOLD, P. 'Blowing the trumpet', *O.F.H.* 3(5), 1984, 176. Memorial of John Taylor, 1744, at Oxford.

Valence

LANKESTER, PHILIP J. 'A military effigy in Dorchester Abbey, Oxon', *Ox.* 52, 1987, 145-72. Perhaps of William de Valence, 1282.

Vampage

PRICE, CORMELL. 'Acrostic brass inscription on the floor in the N. transept of St.Kenelm's, Minster Lovell', *O.A.S.* 47, 1904, 20-22. John Vampage, 1466.

Wilcote

CARTER, W.F. *The Wilcotes monument in Great Tew church.* Reading: Reading Observer, 1907.

Zouch

EVANS, H.F.O. 'The tomb of James Zouch in Oxford Cathedral', *Transactions of the Monumental Brass Society* 9, 1952-62, 509-11. 1503.

10. DIRECTORIES AND MAPS

Directories are an invaluable source for locating people in the past. For the nineteenth century, they are the equivalent of the modern phone book. Many directories for Oxfordshire were published. The list which follows is selective, largely based on volumes I have seen in Oxford or at the British Library, although also drawing on works cited in *English genealogy: an introductory bibliography*. Many Oxfordshire directories are listed in Cordeaux and Merry's bibliographies (above, section 2). The list which follows is in chronological order.

Hunt & Co's City of Oxford directory, including the commercial and private residences in that city and suburbs, and also in the towns of Abingdon, Banbury, Bicester, Deddington, Thame, Witney, Woodstock, &c., &c. ... E. Hunt & Co., 1846.

Post Office directory of Berkshire and Oxfordshire. Kelly & Co., 1847-1939. Title varies; sometimes referred to as *Kelly's directory of Oxfordshire.* Many editions; the Oxfordshire portion was published at various times with different combinations of counties.

Lascelles and Co's directory and gazetteer of the county of Oxford ... Birmingham: Lascelles & Co., 1853.

M. Billing's directory and gazetteer of the counties of Berks and Oxon ... Birmingham: M. Billing, 1854.

Dutton Allen & Co's directory & gazetteer of the counties of Oxon, Berks & Bucks ... Manchester: Dutton Allen & Co., 1863.

The Oxford directory (court, street, trade and commercial) for 1866. Oxford: Wheeler and Day, 1866.

Mathiesons' Oxford directory (including Abingdon) for 1867. Oxford: Wheeler & Day et al for the proprietors, 1867.

Melville and Co's directory of Berkshire, Oxfordshire, Cambridgeshire, Bedfordshire and Northamptonshire ... J. & W. Rider, 1867.

Edward Cassey and Co's history, gazetteer and directory of Berkshire and Oxfordshire. Thomas Danks for the proprietors, 1868.

Websters Oxford, Wallingford, Abingdon and Banbury directory for 1869. Oxford: W.M. Webster, 1869.

Websters Oxford directory including Abingdon, Banbury, Eynsham, Wallingford, Witney and Woodstock; also the principal villages in the vicinity. Oxford: Webster, 1872.

Directories and Maps *continued*

Mercer & Crockers general topographical and historical directory for Oxfordshire. Leicester: Mercer & Crocker, 1874.

J.G. Harrod & Co's royal county directory of Bedfordshire, Buckinghamshire, Berkshire and Oxfordshire. Norwich: Royal County Directory Offices, 1876.

VALTERS, J.C. *Oxford Post Office directory*. Oxford: J.C. Valters, 1880-97. 12 issues. Title varies.

ROWBOTTOM, W. *The Oxford blue book and elector's companion*. Oxford: S. Rowbottom & Son, 1888-90. 3 issues. Includes a rent roll of Oxford city, list of Justices of the Peace for the county, etc.

Kelly's directory of Oxford and neighbourhood. Kelly & Co., 1889- Almost annual, title varies.

Deacons Berkshire, Buckinghamshire and Oxfordshire court guide and county blue book ... 2nd ed. Charles William Deacon, 1890.

Oxford and district trades directory. Edinburgh: Town & County Directories, 1908.

Oxfordshire directory and buyer's guide. Walsall: E.F. Cope & Co., 1910.

The illustrated Oxford year book (University, city and county). Oxford: Holywell Press, 1911-12. 2 issues. Gives names of government, ecclesiastical and educational officers, etc., etc.

Reading, Berks, and Oxford trades directory. Edinburgh: Town & County Directories, 1925.

Berkshire, Buckinghamshire and Oxfordshire directory. Walsall: Aubrey & Co., 1938-40. 4 vols.

Banbury

The Banbury directory. [Banbury]: [ ], 1832.

Rusher's Banbury list. Banbury: J.G. Rusher, 1798-1896. Title varies. Continued by *Pott's original Banbury list and directory*. Banbury: William Potts, 1897-1906.

The directory of Banbury and its neighbourhood. Banbury: G. Walford, 1865.

Kelly's directory of Banbury and neighbourhood. Kelly's Directories, 1932-70. 8 issues.

Burford

Burford almanack, compendium, directory and diary. Burford: Geo. Packer, 1860-1918.

Henley

Kelly's directory of Henley on Thames & neighbourhood. Kelly's Directories, 1932-42. 6 issues.

Heyford

Dew's district almanack. Heyford: J.W. Dew, 1889-92. 3 issues. Heyford district.

Oxford

The Oxford directory, 1861. Oxford: W. Mansell, 1861.

Oxford city directory for 1872. Oxford: Oxford Times, 1872.

G. Shrimpton's Oxford directory. Oxford: G. Shrimpton, 1875-7. 2 issues.

Oxford city and suburban directory for 1876. Oxford: Oxford Times, 1876.

Maps

Directories sometimes, usefully, include maps, which you will need to consult in order to locate particular places. Early maps reveal a great deal about the way in which the landscape has changed in recent times. A number have been recently reprinted:

The old series Ordnance Survey maps of England and Wales ... vol.IV: Central England. Lympne Castle: Harry Margary, 1986. Individual sheet maps of the 1st edition O.S. maps have been reprinted by David & Charles.

HARVEY, P.D.A. 'Banbury', in LOBEL, MARY D., ed. *Historic towns: maps and plans of towns and cities in the British Isles ... vol.1*. Lovell Johns-Cook, Hammond & Kell Organisation, 1969.

SALTER, HERBERT E. *Map of mediaeval Oxford*. O.U.P., 1934.

Old plans of Oxford. O.H.S. 38, 1899. This is accompanied by: HURST, HERBERT. *Oxford topography: an essay*. O.H.S. 39, 1899.

Some manuscript maps are listed in:

COLVIN, H.M. 'Manuscript maps belonging to St.Johns College, Oxford', *Ox*. 15, 1950, 92-103. Lists maps from 10 different counties, but predominantly Oxfordshire and Berkshire.

A manuscript map of Northleigh, which gives the names of inhabitants in 1876, is discussed in:

PERROTT, JOHN. 'Northleigh, 1876', *O.F.H.* 2(9), 1982, 295-7.

Reference must also be made to the sheet map of Oxfordshire parish boundaries published by the Institute of Heraldic and Genealogical Studies. This should be in the possession of every Oxfordshire genealogist. Help in identifying obscure place-names may be had by consulting:

GELLING, MARGARET. *The place-names of Oxfordshire*. 2 vols. English Place-Name Society 23-4, 1953-4.

See also:

ALEXANDER, HENRY. *The place-names of Oxfordshire: their origin and development*. Oxford: Clarendon Press, 1912.

11. OFFICIAL LISTS OF NAMES

Governments are keen on listing their subjects, a trait for which genealogists have cause to be thankful, since the lists which result enable us to locate our ancestors precisely in time and place. Official lists have been compiled for a multitude of reasons: taxation, defence, voting, landownership, etc. A valuable general discussion of these lists, both published and unpublished, is provided by:

GIBSON, JEREMY. 'Locating Oxfordshire surnames', *O.F.H.* **4**(6), 1987, 184-8.

Domesday book is the earliest general listing of manorial lords, and has recently been re-published in a convenient format:

MORRIS, JOHN, ed. *Domesday book, 14. Oxfordshire*. Chichester: Phillimore, 1978.

Many names are listed in the 13th c. hundred rolls. For Oxfordshire, the following have been published:

STONE, E., AND HYDE, PATRICIA, eds. *Oxfordshire hundred rolls of 1279. 1. The Hundred of Bampton. 2. The Borough of Witney*. O.R.S. **46**, 1969.

COOPER, JANET. 'The hundred rolls for the parish of St.Thomas, Oxford', *Ox.* **37**, 1972, 165-76. 1279.

Tax lists

From the medieval period until the seventeenth century, the subsidy provided one of the major sources of government revenue. Each time it was levied, returns of those paying were compiled. Surviving returns are now in the Public Record Office, and most are listed in:

GIBSON, J.S.W. 'Tudor and Stuart subsidies', *O.F.H.* **2**(2), 1980, 37-9.

The subsidy was levied separately on the clergy, and a clerical return for the Diocese of Lincoln (which included Oxfordshire) is printed in:

SALTER, H., ed. *A subsidy collected in the Diocese of Lincoln in 1526*. O.H.S. **63**, 1909.

The Restoration of the Stuart dynasty in 1660 brought with it a search for new sources of finance. Hence the introduction of the hearth tax. All householders in the country (except successful tax dodgers) were listed in the 1665 return:

WEINSTOCK, MAUREEN M.B., ed. *Hearth tax returns, Oxfordshire, 1665*. O.R.S. **21**, 1940. This is indexed in: GEERE, JEREMY. *Index to Oxfordshire hearth tax 1665*. Church Hanborough: Oxfordshire Family History Society, 1985.

The next financial innovation of importance for the genealogist was the land tax, introduced in 1696, although there are few surviving returns prior to the late 18th century. A complete list of those that do survive is to be found in:

GIBSON, J.S.W. 'Land tax assessments for Oxfordshire', *O.F.H.* **3**(1), 1983, 18-22.

A number of works bring together collections of tax returns etc. for particular places:

Banbury

GIBSON, J.S.W. 'Taxpayers in Restoration Banbury', *C.&Ch.* **9**, 1984, 168-88. Collates returns from the 'free and voluntary present', 1661, the hearth tax, 1662 and 1665, and the subsidy, 1663, with notes from wills and the parish register, etc.

Great Rollright

BAUGHEN, CLIFF. 'Land tax assessment: Great Rollright', *O.F.H.* **4**(2), 1986, 60. List of surnames in assessments, 1785-1831.

Oxford

ROGERS, J.E. THOROLD, ed. *Oxford city documents, financial and judicial, 1268-1665*. O.H.S. **18**, 1891. Includes poll tax 1380-81, hearth tax 1665, calendar of documents, 1313-1630, rental of 1317-18, etc.

SALTER, H.E. 'Subsidies and taxes', *O.H.S.* **75**, 1923, 138-353. Oxford returns for the subsidies of 1543, 1544, 1648 and 1667, the hearth tax, 1665, and the poll tax, 1667.

Wheatley

HASSALL, W.O. *Wheatley records, 956-1956*. O.R.S. **37**, 1956. Includes numerous documents, e.g. subsidy rolls, 1305-6 and 1524/5, list of communicants, 1612/13, hearth tax, 1662, will of Abraham Archdale, 1631, extracts from directories, etc., etc.

Woodstock

HALLISSEY, MARY, AND SHIPP, JACK. 'The inhabitants of early seventeenth century Woodstock', *O.L.H.* **3**(6), 1991, 240-50. Discussion of a series of listings of inhabitants, 17th c.

Oath rolls

In 1641, as civil war loomed, Parliament required all adult males to take an oath of loyalty, known as the 'protestation'. Everyone had to sign the oath; consequently, the signatures, or marks, of a large proportion of the population in 1641/2 are now preserved in the House of Lords Record Office. Those for Oxfordshire are printed in:

Official Lists of Names continued

Oath rolls *continued*

DOBSON, CHRISTOPHER S.A. *Oxfordshire protestation returns, 1641-2.* O.R.S. **36**, 1955. This is indexed in:

DE JONG, GWYN. *Index to the Oxfordshire Protestation oath returns.* Witney: Oxfordshire Family History Society, 1993.

See also:

GOADBY, F.R.L. 'Protestation returns 1641-42: Caversham', *O.F.H.* **3**(7), 1985, 229-30. Lists found in parish registers, probably made for the protestation. Gives many names.

A similar oath was taken in 1695, and returns for Banbury and Woodstock have been published:

GIBSON, J.S.W. 'Some Banbury inhabitants in the 1690s', *C.&Ch.* **10**(4), 1986, 82-90. Lists signatories of the Association Oath roll 1695, with notes from the parish register, wills, etc.

GIBSON, J.S.W. 'Some Woodstock inhabitants in 1696', *O.F.H.* **4**(2), 1986, 38-41. The Association Oath roll for the borough.

Poll books

When Parliamentary elections were contested, lists of voters were sometimes published, showing how votes were cast. Generally, only one or two copies of these poll books survive, and they are not listed here. For full details see Cordeaux and Merry's bibliographies (above, section 2) and the works cited in *English genealogy: an introductory bibliography.* Parts of the 1754 poll book for the county have been published in modern editions:

DANNATT, G.H. *The Oxfordshire election of 1754.* Record publication **6**. Oxford: Oxfordshire County Council, 1970. Includes extracts from the poll book for Shillingford, Warborough, Ardley and Bicester, with other miscellaneous documents.

GIBSON, J.S.W. 'The 1754 election in North Oxfordshire', *C.&Ch.* **11**(8), 183-213. Includes 1754 poll book for the Hundreds of Banbury and Bloxham; also list of freeholders in Banbury Hundred prepared for canvassers' use.

Census returns

By far the most useful lists are those deriving from the official censuses. These began in 1801, but normally the earliest surviving returns of genealogical value are those for 1841. For Oxfordshire, a number of stray earlier returns are also available. Works on the census are listed chronologically.

1801

SMITH, DONNETTE S. '1801 census of Stoke Lyne', *O.F.H.* **1**(9), 1979, 240. Surnames only.

1821

SCARR, JACK. 'Parishioners at Wolvercote, Oxford, in May 1821', *O.F.H.* **3**(3), 1983, 104. Census listing.

1832

WALL, RICHARD. 'The inhabitants of Summertown, Oxford, in the year 1832', *Local population studies* **28**, 1982, 81-8. Discussion of a local census, with some extracts.

1841

CHINNOR HISTORICAL AND ARCHAEOLOGICAL SOCIETY. *Notes on the population of Emmington 1086-1914 (with particular reference to the period 1841-72).* Occasional paper **4**. Chinnor: the Society, 1979. Includes transcripts of census returns, 1841-71, list of landowners from the 1841 tithe map, voters lists, 1903-12, etc.

SCHUMER, BERYL. 'Census families at North Leigh', *O.F.H.* **1**(4), 1978, 100. Lists surnames found in 1841 and 1851 censuses.

1851

The major published index of Oxfordshire censuses is:

KEARSEY, HUGH. *Index to Oxfordshire census, 1851.* Oxford: Oxfordshire F.H.S., 1990-91. v.1. Henley Union. v.2. Thame Union. v.3. Wallingford Union. v.4. Headington, inc. parts of Oxford city. v.5. Bicester Union. v.6. Woodstock Union. v.7. Witney Union. v.8. Chipping Norton Union. v.9. Banbury Union. v.10. Abingdon Union. v.11. Brackley, Wycombe and Bradfield Unions. v.12. Oxford City.

See also:

BETTERIDGE, PAUL. *Index to Oxford city census 1851.* Oxford: Oxfordshire Family History Society, 1986.

GIBSON, JEREMY. 'The 1851 census project', *O.F.H.* **2**(6), 1981, 171-87. Discussion of the project, including a summarised transcript for Church Hanborough.

GIBSON, JEREMY. 'A county transcription of the 1851 census', *O.L.H.* **1**(4), 1982, 15-30. Description of a major project, with extract from Church Hanborough.

GIBSON, J.S.W. 'The 1851 census for Oxfordshire', *O.F.H.* **2**(3), 1980, 73-77. Lists returns available at the Centre for Oxfordshire Studies.

1851 continued

GRANT, C. JOHN. 'North Newington census surname index: returns for 1851-61-71-81, including boarders, lodgers and visitors', *O.F.H.* **4**(4), 1987, 131-2. See also **4**(8), 1988, 246-8 (which also includes index for Shutford).

GIBSON, J.S.W. 'From North Oxfordshire to Northampton', *C.&Ch.* **10**(9), 242-3. Lists migrants from North Oxfordshire found in the 1851 census for Northampton.

TRINDER, BARRIE S. 'Banbury's poor in 1850', *C.&Ch.* **3**(6), 1966, 83-128. Includes a street by street survey of the poor, with many names, partly based on 1851 census.

1861

CHINNOR HISTORICAL AND ARCHAEOLOGICAL SOCIETY. *Oakley people: a commentary on a mid-Victorian community.* Occasional paper 7. Chinnor: the Society, [198-]. Includes transcript of 1861 census, with biographical notes; also lists owners and tenants from the 1859 tithe award.

1881

The Mormons are currently preparing a microfiche index to the 1881 census. This will be an essential tool for every genealogist. In the meantime, see:

NEWBIGGING, CAROLE. 'An item from the 1881 census for Cowley', *O.F.H.* **3**(3), 1983, 105-6. See also **3**(5), 1984, 169-70. Lists residents at a military college.

Landowners' Census

A different type of census was taken in 1873. Everyone who owned more than one acre of land was listed, and the return for Oxfordshire was published as:

Return of owners of land, 1873: Oxfordshire. House of Commons parliamentary papers, 1874, 72, pt.2, 95-117. Reprinted Oxfordshire Family History Society, 1993.

The church formerly had a much more important role in society than it does today. The importance of this fact for the genealogist is that many essential sources—for example, parish registers, probate records, local government records, etc.— are to be found in ecclesiastical rather than state archives. Works on ecclesiastical sources are listed throughout this bibliography; here the emphasis is on those topics which are primarily to do with the administration of the church. Useful background is provided by three works:

MARSHALL, E. *Oxford.* Diocesan histories. S.P.C.K., 1882. Includes list of bishops.

BOWKER, MARGARET. *The secular clergy in the Diocese of Lincoln, 1495-1520.* Cambridge: Cambridge U.P., 1968. Includes various lists of clergy.

MCCLATCHEY, DIANA. *Oxfordshire clergy 1777-1869: a study of the established church and of the role of its clergy in local society.* Oxford: Clarendon Press, 1960.

In the medieval period, Oxfordshire was in the Diocese of Lincoln. Consequently, some documents relating to the county are still at Lincoln. For these, see:

JOHNSON, C.P.C. 'Some Oxfordshire genealogical sources at the Lincolnshire Archives Office', *O.F.H.* **2**(4), 1981, 104-6. This primarily lists medieval records of Lincoln Diocese, including probate records, accounts, clergy lists, etc. For a full listing of Lincoln records, consult:

MAJOR, KATHLEEN. *A handlist of the records of the Bishop of Lincoln, and of the Archdeacons of Lincoln and Stow.* O.U.P., 1953.

The most important ecclesiastical source for the medieval period are the bishops' registers, which record the general business of the diocese. The lists of ordinations and institutions they contain, together with the occasional will, are of particular value to genealogists. Published registers for the Diocese of Lincoln containing substantial Oxfordshire material include:

PHILLIMORE, W.P.W., ed. *Rotuli Hugonis de Welles, episcopi Lincolniensis A.D. MCCIX-MCCXXXV.* 3 vols. Lincoln Record Society **3**, **6**, & **9**. Final vol. ed. F.N. Davis. Also published as Canterbury and York Society **1**, **3**, & **4**. Vol.2 includes institutions in the Oxford Archdeaconry.

DAVIS, F.N., ed. *Rotuli Roberti Grosseteste, episcopi Lincolniensis, A.D. MCCXXXV-MCCLIII, necnon, Rotulus Henrici de Lexington, episcopi Lincolniensis, A.D. MCCLIV-MCCLIX.* Lincoln Record Society **11**, 1914. Also published as Canterbury and York Society **10**.

DAVIS, F.N., ET AL, eds. *Rotuli Ricardi Gravesend, Episcopi Lincolniensis, A.D. MCCLVIII-MCCLXXIX.* Lincoln Record Society **20**, 1925. Also published as Canterbury and York Society **31**. Includes many Oxfordshire institutions.

HILL, ROSALIND M.T., ed. *The rolls and register of Bishop Oliver Sutton 1280-1299, vols.III-VII: Memoranda.* Lincoln Record Society **48, 52, 60, 64, & 69.** 1954-75.

ARCHER, MARGARET, ed. *The register of Bishop Philip Repingdon, 1405-1419.* 3 vols. Lincoln Record Society **57-8, & 74,** 1963-82. Includes wills.

See also:

CLARK, ANDREW, ed. *Lincoln Diocese documents, 1450-1544.* Early English Text Society **149**. Kegan Paul, Trench, Trubner & Co., 1914.

THOMPSON, A. HAMILTON, ed. *Visitations of religious houses in the Diocese of Lincoln.* Lincoln Record Society **7, 14, & 21,** 1914-29. Also published as Canterbury and York Society **17, 24, & 33.** 15th c., includes information on founders.

THOMPSON, A. HAMILTON, ed. *Visitations in the Diocese of Lincoln, 1517-1531.* 3 vols. Lincoln Record Society **33, 35, & 37,** 1940-44. Gives many names of Oxfordshire clergy.

SALTER, H. 'A visitation of Oxfordshire in 1540', *O.A.S.* **75**, 1930, 289-307. Ecclesiastical visitation, many names.

BASKERVILLE, G. 'The dispossessed religious of Oxfordshire', *O.A.S.* **75**, 1930, 327-47. Lists pensioners. Includes will of Richard King, 16th c. (undated).

The Diocese of Oxford was established at the Reformation, and included Berkshire and Buckinghamshire as well as Oxfordshire. A number of works relating to the ecclesiastical courts and their records are worth consulting:

HOWARD-DRAKE, JACK. *Oxford church courts: depositions, 1542-1550.* Oxford: Oxfordshire archives, 1992.

TURNER, W.H. 'Ecclesiastical court books of the Diocese of Oxford', *O.A.H.S.P.* N.S. **3**, 1880, 130-39. General discussion of contents.

BRINKWORTH, E.R., ed. *The Archdeacon's court: liber actorum, 1584.* 2 vols. O.R.S. **23-4**, 1942-6. Includes notes on the clergy.

See also:

BRINKWORTH, E.R. 'The study and use of Archdeacon's court records, illustrated from the Oxford records (1566-1759)', *Transactions of the Royal Historical Society* 4th series **25**, 1943, 93-119, and under Eynsham below.

BRINKWORTH, E.R.C. 'Cases from the peculiar court of Banbury', *C.&Ch.* **1**, 1962, 148-53. 17-18th c., general discussion.

The names of many churchmen, clerical and lay, are to be found in:

SHARPE, FREDERICK. *The church bells of Oxfordshire.* 4 vols. O.R.S. **28, 30, 32 & 34.** 1949-53.

The clergy of the diocese in 1559 are listed, with biographical notes, in a series of articles by S.S. Pearce:

PEARCE, S. SPENCER. 'The clergy of the Deaneries of Chipping Norton and Deddington, and the peculiars of Banbury and Cropredy during the settlement of 1559 and afterwards', *O.A.S.*, 1916, 15-86.

PEARCE, S. SPENCER. 'The clergy of the Deanery of Cuddesdon, and of the peculiars of Langford, Thame and Great Milton during the settlement of 1559 and afterwards', *O.A.S.*, **1920**, 242-89.

PEARCE, S. SPENCER. 'The clergy of the Deaneries of Henley and Aston and of the peculiar of Dorchester during the settlement of 1559 and afterwards', *O.A.S.*, 1918, 127-89.

PEARCE, S. SPENCER. 'The clergy of the Rural Deanery of Oxford and of the peculiar of Newington with Britewell, at the time of the settlement of 1559 and afterwards', *O.A.S.*, **1919**, 198-234.

PEARCE, S. SPENCER. 'The clergy of the Deaneries of Witney and Bicester during the settlement of 1559 and afterwards', *O.A.S.* **60**, 1914, 180-237.

PEARCE, S. SPENCER. 'The clergy of the Woodstock Deanery and the settlement of 1559', *O.A.S.* **58**, 1912, 89-110. Includes biographical notes.

A number of works provide the names of clergy at later dates:

PEARCE, S. SPENCER. 'A certificate of the Oxford clergy, A.D. 1593', *O.A.S.* **59**, 1913, 145-70. Many names; covers the whole Diocese.

MARSHALL, WILLIAM M. 'Episcopal activity in the Hereford and Oxford dioceses, 1660-1760', *Midland history* **8**, 1983, 106-20. General discussion of ordinations, confirmations and visitations.

JUKES, H.A. LLOYD, ed. *Articles of enquiry addressed to the clergy of the Diocese of Oxford at the primary visitation of Dr. Thomas Secker, 1738.* O.R.S. **38**, 1957. Includes names of clergy.

TILLER, KATE, ed. *Church and chapel in Oxfordshire 1851: the return of the census of religious worship.* O.R.S. **55**, 1987. Gives names of clergy or lay officers making the returns.

BAKER, E.P., ed. *Bishop Wilberforce's visitation returns, for the Archdeaconry of Oxford in the year 1854.* O.R.S. **35**, [1954]. Gives names of clergy.

Brief notes on many clergy with Oxfordshire connections are included, despite its title, in:
LONGDEN, HENRY ISHAM. *Northamptonshire and Rutland clergy from 1500.* 16 vols. in 6. Northampton: Archer & Goodman, 1938-52.

Many histories of particular churches have been compiled, and frequently include clergy lists, the names of churchwardens, monumental inscriptions, parish register extracts, etc. These cannot be listed here; reference should be made to Cordeaux and Merry's bibliographies (above, section 2). Lists of clergy in particular churches, together with other miscellaneous information, are to be found in:

Deddington Deanery

WALKER, G.G. *Churches of the Banbury area: drawings of the churches in the Deanery of Deddington and some others.* Kineton: Roundwood Press, 1975. Includes brief notes on each church, but little on monuments.

Eynsham

WRIGHT, LILIAN. '1584', *Eynsham record* **1**, 1984, 22-6. Discussion of Archdeacons' court records relating to Eynsham.

Great Haseley

WEARE, T.W. *Some remarks upon the church of Great Hasely ... together with copious extracts from Delafield's ms. ... entitled Notitia Hasleiana.* 2nd ed. Oxford: John Henry Parker for the Society for Promoting the Study of Gothic Architecture, 1848. Includes notes on rectors, with list of monuments, brasses, arms, etc.

Kingham

MANN, RALPH. *The rectors of Kingham.* Kingham: G. Papworth, 1990.

Marston

CLARK, G.N. 'Marston church, near Oxford', *O.A.S.* **75**, 1930, 263-87. Includes list of vicars.

Oxford

FLETCHER, W.G. DIMOCK. *The black friars of Oxford.* Oxford: Oxford Chronicle Co., 1882. Includes list of priors.

LITTLE, ANDREW G. *The Grey Friars in Oxford. Part 1: A history of the Convent. Part 2: Biographical notices, together with appendices of original documents.* O.H.S. **20**, 1892.

Pyrton

WIGGINS, C.A. *Vicars of Pyrton and Shirburn in the Diocese of Oxford.* Pyrton: the author, 1947.

Shirburn

See Pyrton

Westcot Barton

MARSHALL, J. *Memorials of Westcott Barton.* John Russell Smith, 1870. Includes list of rectors and brief notes on memorials.

Witney

NORRIS, W. FOXLEY. 'Memoranda relating to Witney, Oxon', *Journal of the British Archaeological Association* **47**, 1891, 120-23. List of rectors with brief biographical notes.

Nonconformists

Many denominations have been active in Oxfordshire, and much has been published on the histories of particular churches. The following list is not comprehensive; rather it attempts to identify works likely to be of particular interest to genealogists. Two useful works on nonconformity in general are provided by:

CLAPINSON, MARY, ed. *Bishop Fell and nonconformity: visitation documents from the Oxford Diocese, 1682-83.* O.R.S. **52**, 1980. Includes a return of 'conventicles', 1669, list of dissenters, 1683, and letters from many clergy giving both their own names and those of nonconformists.

TRINDER, B.S. 'Schisms and divisions: the origins of dissenting congregations in Banbury, 1772-1860', *C.&Ch.* **8**(8), 1982, 207-21. Includes references to potentially useful sources.

Baptists

HAYDEN, P. 'The Baptists in Oxford, 1656-1819', *Baptist quarterly* **29**, 1981, 127-36. Includes many references to potentially useful sources.

TRINDER, BARRIE S. 'The radical Baptists', *C.&Ch.* **2**, 1962-5, 179-92. Banbury. Notes various potentially useful sources.

Congregationalists

SUMMERS, W.H. *History of the Congregational churches in the Berks, South Oxon and South Bucks Association, with notes on the earlier nonconformist history of the district.* Newbury: W.J. Blacket, 1905. Brief histories of many individual churches, giving names of ministers, etc.

Jews

ROTH, CECIL. *The Jews of medieval Oxford.* O.H.S. N.S. **9**, 1951. Includes lists of names, 1194-1290.

ROTH, CECIL. 'Jews in Oxford after 1290', *Ox.* **15**, 1950, 63-80.

ROTH, CECIL. 'The starrs of Oxford', *Ox.* **22**, 1957, 63-77. Discussion of Jewish business documents.

NEUBAUER, A. 'Notes on the Jews in Oxford', *O.H.S.* **16**, 1890, 277-316. 12-13th c., includes deed extracts.

DANN, URIEL. 'Jews in 18th-century Oxford: further observations', *Ox.* **54**, 1989, 345-53.

Methodists

OXLEY, J.E. *A history of Wesley Memorial Church, Oxford, 1818-1968.* Oxford: [the Church]: 1968. Includes list of ministers.

Presbyterians

TYSSEN, AMHERST D. 'The presbyterians of Bloxham and Milton near Banbury in Oxfordshire', *Transactions of the Unitarian Historical Society* **2**, 1920, 9-32. Many names, including those of the original trustees, 1708.

Quakers

COTTIS, JANIE. 'Quaker records for Oxfordshire family historians', *O.F.H.* **5**(7), 1991, 286-92. To be continued.

PAUL, E.D. 'The records of the Banbury monthly meeting of the Society of Friends', *Ox.* **31**, 1966, 163-5. 17-20th c.

TRINDER, B. 'The origins of Quakerism in Banbury', *C.&Ch.* **7**(9), 1979, 263-9. Includes some names.

Roman Catholics

DAVIDSON, ALAN. 'Oxfordshire recusancy, 1580-1640', *C.&Ch.* **5**(9), 1974, 167-75. Mentions many Oxfordshire families.

STAPLETON, MRS. BRYAN. *A history of the post-Reformation Catholic missions in Oxfordshire with an account of the families connected with them.* Henry Frowde, 1906. Includes lists of clergy, etc.

'Recusants in Oxfordshire, 1603-1633', *O.A.S.* **69**, 1924, 7-71. Lists.

13. ESTATE AND FAMILY PAPERS

A. *GENERAL*

The records of estate administration—deeds, leases, rentals, surveys, accounts, etc.—are a mine of information for the genealogist. Many of these records have been published in full or part, although far more still lie untouched in the archives. A number of general collections of deeds have been published in abstract or index form:

SALTER, H.E., ed. *The feet of fines for Oxfordshire, 1195-1291.* O.R.S. **12**, 1930. Feet of fines are medieval deeds.

'Palaeography, genealogy and topography', *Topographical quarterly* **7**, 1938-9, 66-93. Deed abstracts compiled from a bookseller's collection.

HASSALL, W.O., ed. *Index of persons in Oxfordshire deeds acquired by the Bodleian Library, 1878-1963.* O.R.S. **45**, 1966. Provides brief notes on several thousand persons named. Very useful.

The process of enclosing land from open fields resulted in the creation of many documents. Enclosure awards usually include complete lists of owners and tenants, and are consequently invaluable for genealogists. Awards for Oxfordshire are listed in:

A handlist of inclosure acts and awards relating to the county of Oxford. 2nd ed. Record publication **2**. Oxford: Oxfordshire County Council, 1975. This includes a list of awards for that part of Berkshire transferred to Oxfordshire in 1974. It supersedes:

County of Oxford: Inclosure awards enrolled in the office of the clerk of the peace of the county, or at Westminster. Oxford: [Clerk of the Peace], 1869.

A few private families have preserved collections of estate documents relating to wider areas than one parish. Works relating to two such collections are available:

G[IBSON], J.S.W. 'Two Oxfordshire manorial court books', *C.&Ch.* **4**, 1968-71, 160. Brief note on 16-17th c. manorial records of the Pope family of Wroxton Abbey, relating to North Oxfordshire.

Estate and Family Papers *continued*

SALTER, H.E. *The Boarstall cartulary.* O.H.S. **88**, 1930. Calendar of the private cartulary of Edmund Rede of Boarstall, Buckinghamshire, drawn up in 1444, and including deeds relating to Checkenden, Standhill, and Gatehampton in Oxfordshire, Wallingford and Clopcot in Berkshire, as well as Boarstall. Also includes Rede's will, 1489, and a list of knights of the Honour of Wallingford, 1300.

The estate records of the colleges of Oxford University are generally of national rather than Oxfordshire significance, and publications based on them will in due course be listed in a volume devoted to the ancient Universities. However, their properties did include Oxfordshire manors; notes on estate administration at New College form the subject of:

RICKARD, R.L., ed. *The progress notes of Warden Woodward round the Oxfordshire estates of New College, Oxford 1659-1675.* O.R.S. **27**, [1949]. Notes on the administration of estates at Adderbury, Heyford, Kingham, Stanton St.John, and Swalcliffe.

B. *ECCLESIASTICAL CARTULARIES*

In the medieval period, a great deal of property was owned by ecclesiastical institutions such as churches, monasteries, dioceses, etc. Ecclesiastical estate records have survived much better than those of private families, and many are in print. For Oxfordshire, these include:

Eynsham

SALTER, H.E., ed. *Eynsham cartulary.* 2 vols. O.H.S. **49** & **51**, 1907-8.

Godstow

CLARK, ANDREW, ed. *The English register of Godstow nunnery, near Oxford, written about 1450.* 3 vols. Early English Text Society original series **129-30** & **142**, 1905-11. Relating to estates largely in Oxfordshire, but also in neighbouring counties.

Goring

COOKE, A.H., ed. 'A rent roll of the suppressed priory of Goring, 1546', *Berkshire archaeological journal* **35**, 1931, 120-23.

Oseney

CLARK, ANDREW, ed. *The English register of Oseney Abbey, by Oxford, written about 1460.* 2 vols. Early English Text Society original series **133** & **144**, 1907-13.

SALTER, H.E., ed. *Cartulary of Oseney Abbey.* 6 vols. O.H.S. **89-91**, **97-8** & **101**, 1929-36.

Oseney *continued*

POSTLES, DAVID. 'The manorial accounts of Oseney Abbey 1274-1348', *Archives* **14**(62), 1979, 75-80. General discussion; the Abbey had estates in Oxfordshire and Buckinghamshire.

Oxford. St.Frideswide

WIGRAM, SPENCER ROBERT, ed. *The cartulary of the monastery of St.Frideswide at Oxford.* 2 vols. O.H.S. **28** & **31**, 1895-6. Vol.1. General and city charters. Vol.2. The chantry and country parish charters.

Oxford. St.John the Baptist

SALTER, H.E., ed. *A cartulary of the hospital of St.John the Baptist.* O.H.S. **66** & **68-9**, 1914-17. Primarily concerned with property in Oxford; medieval-19th c.

Sandford

LEYS, AGNES M., ed. *The Sandford cartulary.* 2 vols. O.R.S. **19** & **22**, 1938-41. 12-13th c. Vol.2 includes many deeds from adjacent counties.

Thame

SALTER, H.E., ed. *The Thame cartulary.* 2 vols. O.R.S. **25-6**, 1947-8.

Ecclesiastical institutions in other counties also owned much Oxfordshire property. See:

Lincoln Cathedral

FOSTER, C.W. ed. *The registrum antiquissimum of the Cathedral church of Lincoln.* Lincoln Record Society **27-9**, 1931-35. Register of medieval deeds, including many from Oxfordshire. Many further volumes have been published, but they contain few Oxfordshire deeds.

Windsor. St.George's Chapel

DALTON, JOHN NEALE, ed. *The manuscripts of St.George's Chapel, Windsor.* Windsor: the Dean and Chapter, 1957. Relating to property in 18 Oxfordshire villages, as well as to estates in many other counties.

B. *MANORIAL RECORDS AND DESCENTS, etc.*

Bampton

G., H. 'The manor of Bampton, and family of Horde', *Topographer & genealogist* **2**, 1853, 515-20. Medieval deeds; notes on the family, 16-17th c.

WILLIAMS, BENJAMIN. 'Additional remarks on the hide of land, and on some ancient manorial customs in Oxfordshire', *Archaeologia* **35**, 1854, 470-74. Includes customary of Bampton, with names of 'substantial inhabitants', 1593.

Broughton Castle

SLADE, H. GORDON. 'Broughton Castle, Oxfordshire', *Archaeological journal* **135**, 1978, 138-94. Includes pedigree showing descent through Wykeham, Fiennes, and Twisleton, 14-19th c., also pedigrees of Broughton, 13-14th c., and Danvers and Fermor, 16th c.

Chalford

See Dean

Checkendon

COOKE, A.H. 'Some early Checkendon documents', *B.B.O.A.J.* **32**, 1928, 1-7 & 53-62. Calendar of 19 medieval deeds.

Chibenhurst

See Chislehampton

Chislehampton

BAYLEY, W. D'OYLY, ed. 'Ancient deeds', *Topographer & genealogist* **2**, 1853, 340-44. Relating to Chislehampton and Chibenhurst.

Cornbury

WATNEY, VERNON J. *Cornbury and the Forest of Wychwood*. Hatchards, 1910. Includes a 'list of tenants occupiers and owners', and shows descent through many families, e.g. Beauchamp, Dudley, Fortescue, Danvers, Hyde, Spencer, etc.

Cuxham

HARVEY, P.D.A., ed. *Manorial records of Cuxham, Oxfordshire, circa 1200-1359*. O.R.S. **50**, 1976. Also published in the Historical Manuscripts Commission's joint publications series **23**. A model edition, including numerous charters, terriers and lists of tenants, account rolls, court rolls and tax assessments, with a detailed listing of unpublished pre-1360 records and persons named in them.

Dean

LOBEL, M.D. *The history of Dean and Chalford*. O.R.S. **17**, 1935. Includes list of manorial tenants, 16-19th c., medieval deeds, lay subsidy returns, 1316, 1327 and 1545-6, and hearth tax, 1662, with a descent of the manor.

Emmington

CHINNOR HISTORICAL AND ARCHAEOLOGICAL SOCIETY. *The fields of Emmington*. Occasional paper **5**. Chinnor: the Society, [198-?]. Includes various lists of tenants, 1697-1841.

Eynsham

ATKINS, BRIAN. 'John Whiting's survey of Eynsham, 1650, part 1: the village', *Eynsham record* **6**, 1989, 40-50. Lists tenants.

RICHARDS, PAMELA. 'The Eynsham Mansard House: a story of a property', *Eynsham record* **4**, 1987, 35-40. See also **5**, 1988, 45-6. Traces descent of an Eynsham house, 17-20th c.

Finstock

WALTON, HILARY. 'Finstock copyholders, 1584-1772', *O.F.H.* **1**(7), 1979, 180-82. Includes list of surnames.

Goring

GAMBIER-PERRY, T.R., ed. *A collection of charters relating to Goring, Streatley, and the neighbourhood, 1181-1546, preserved in the Bodleian Library*. O.R.S. **13-14**, 1931-2. Includes many grants to the Loveday family and notes on other principal families.

Great Milton

HARVEY, JOHN R. 'Great Milton, Oxfordshire, and Thorncroft, Surrey: the building accounts for two manor-houses of the late fifteenth century', *Journal of the British Archaeological Association* 3rd series **18**, 1955, 42-56. Includes many names.

Great Rollright

JEFFERY, REGINALD W. *The manors and advowsons of Great Rollright*. O.R.S. **9**, 1927. Includes terrier, 1662, a descent of the manor, an account of the rectors, and a list of those who served in the armed forces, 1914-19.

Hampden

SOUCH, ERNEST E., AND SOUCH, DEBORAH. 'Hampden manor: where local history and archaeology meet', *O.L.H.* **2**(7), 1987, 255-65. Includes descent of the manor.

Hampton Poyle

GREENFIELD, BENJAMIN WYATT. 'The descent of the manor of Hampton-Poyle in the county of Oxford, from the extinction of the family of De La Pole in the early part of the fifteenth century; in the families of Gaynesford, Bury, Dormer, Hawtrey and Croke, illustrated with genealogical tables and with original documents', *Herald & genealogist* **1**, 1863, 209-24 & 321-44. See also **3**, 1866, 306-7.

GREENFIELD, BENJAMIN WYATT. 'Descent of the manor and advowson of Hampton Poyle, in the county of Oxford, in the family of West, from 1648 to 1712', *Herald & genealogist* **3**, 1866, 297-306. Includes pedigree.

Estate and Family Papers continued

Haseley
See Pirton

Islip
HARVEY, BARBARA F., ed. 'Custumal (1391) and bye-laws (1386-1540) of the manor of Islip', *O.R.S.* **40**, 1959, 80-119. Many names.

Kingston Blount
'Descent of the manor of Kingston Blount', *M.G.H.* 5th series **9**, 1929-31, 315-25. Medieval.

Kirtlington
GRIFFITHS, MATTHEW. 'Kirtlington manor court, 1500-1650', *Ox.* **45**, 1980, 260-83. General discussion.

Marston
CLARK, G.N. 'Enclosure by agreement at Marston, near Oxford', *English historical review* **42**, 1927, 87-94. Gives names of tenants.

Minster Lovell
HASSALL, W.O. 'Minster Lovell in 1602', *Ox.* **10**, 1945, 101-4. Survey listing tenants.

North Leigh
SCHUMER, BERYL. 'Manorial records', *O.F.H.* **3**(1), 1983, 6-8. General discussion of their genealogical uses, partially based on those for North Leigh.

SCHUMER, BERYL. 'An Elizabethan survey of North Leigh, Oxfordshire', *Ox.* **40**, 1975, 309-24. The survey is not transcribed, but many surnames of tenants, 1581-1657, are given.

Oxford
SALTER, H.E., ed. 'A calendar of the deeds about Oxford that are preserved at Bridgwater', *O.H.S.* **80**, 1924, 216-66. 15th c. deeds.

SALTER, H.E., ed. *Oxford city properties*. O.H.S. **83**, 1926. Includes various rentals, 1606-1835, histories of properties giving many names of owners and occupiers, licences for signs, 1587-1766, wine licences, 1592-1731, etc.

SALTER, H.E., ed. *The Oxford deeds of Balliol College*. O.H.S. **64**, 1913. Medieval-19th c.

SALTER, H.E. *Survey of Oxford*. ed. W.A. Pantin. O.H.S. N.S. **14** & **20**, 1960-69. Traces the descent of most Oxford tenements, 12-19th c.

DODGSON, E.O. 'Notes on nos. 56, 58, 60, 62 and 64, Banbury Road', *Ox.* **32**, 1967, 53-9. Includes names of builders and early (19th c.) occupiers.

Pirton
PEARMAN, M.T. 'The descent of the manors of Pirton and Haseley', *O.A.S.* **27**, 1892, 1-24.

Somerton
BALLARD, A. 'Seven Somerton court rolls', *O.A.S.* **50**, 1906, 1-27. 16th c.

Streatley
See Goring

Watlington
PEARMAN, M.T. 'A Watlington court roll of the 15th century', *O.A.S.* **44**, 1902, 16-19. Brief description.

West Adderbury
BEESON, C.F.C. 'Halle Place in West Adderbury and its occupants', *C.&Ch.* **2**, 1962-5, 199-206. Traces descent of the property, 15-20th c., mentioning the Goylen, Pett, Barber and Risley families, etc.

HOBSON, T.F. *Adderbury 'rectoria': the manor at Adderbury belonging to New College, Oxford: the building of the chancel, 1408-18; account rolls, deeds, and court rolls.* O.R.S. **8**, 1926. Account rolls, 1408-19.

Woodstock
MARSHALL, EDWARD. *The early history of Woodstock Manor and its environs in Bladon, Hensington, New Woodstock, Blenheim, with later notices.* Oxford: James Parker & Co., 1873. Supplement, 1874. Includes descent of the manor, deeds, list of rectors, mayors and M.P's of Woodstock, etc.

14. RECORDS OF NATIONAL, COUNTY AND LOCAL ADMINISTRATION

A. *NATIONAL AND COUNTY*

Most of Oxfordshire's leading families have sent a member to represent the county or a borough in Parliament. Biographical information on Oxfordshire members of parliament is contained in:

WILLIAMS, W.R.J. *The Parliamentary history of the county of Oxford, including the city and University of Oxford, and the boroughs of Banbury, Burford, Chipping Norton, Dadington, Witney and Woodstock ... 1213-1899, with biographical and genealogical notices of the members.* Brecknock: Edwin Davies, 1899.

See also:

TATE, W.E. 'Members of Parliament and their personal relations to enclosures: a study with special reference to Oxfordshire enclosures, 1757-1843', *Agricultural history* **23**, 1949, 213-20. Includes a list of MP's concerned in Oxfordshire enclosures.

Reference should also be made to section 7 of *English genealogy: an introductory bibliography.*

MP's, with other officers, are also listed in:

DAVENPORT, JOHN MARRIOTT. *Oxfordshire annals.* Oxford: [ ], 1869. Lists members of parliament, chairmen of quarter sessions from 1771, clerks of the peace from 1684, etc.

DAVENPORT, JOHN MARRIOTT. *Oxfordshire: lords lieutenant, high sheriffs and members of parliament, &c.* Revised by Thomas Marriott Davenport. Oxford: Clarendon Press, 1888.

Official lists of names, such as tax lists and census schedules, have already been discussed. There are, however, many other records of central and county government which provide information of genealogical value; these are listed here in rough chronological order.

COOPER, JANET, ed. *The Oxfordshire eyre, 1241.* O.R.S. **56**, 1989.

GRAHAM, ROSE, ed. 'Description of Oxford from the hundred rolls, A.D. 1279', *O.H.S.* **47**, 1905, 1-98. Lists holders of land by knight service.

SALTER, H.E. *Records of mediaeval Oxford: coroners inquests, the walls of Oxford, etc.* Oxford: Oxford Chronicle Co., 1912. Coroners inquests, 1296-1389.

HAMMER, C.I. 'Patterns of homicide in a medieval university town: fourteenth-century Oxford', *Past & present* **78**, 1978, 3-23. General discussion, based on the previous work.

KIMBALL, ELISABETH G., ed. *Oxfordshire sessions of the peace in the reign of Richard II.* O.R.S. **53**, 1983.

LEADAM, I.S., ed. *The Domesday of inclosures, 1517-1518: being the extant returns to Chancery for Berks., Bucks., Cheshire, Essex, Leicestershire, Lincolnshire, Northants., Essex, and Warwickshire, by the Commissioners of Inclosures in 1517 and for Bedfordshire in 1518, together with Dugdale's ms. notes of the Warwickshire inquisitions in 1517, 1518 and 1549.* 2 vols. Longmans Green & Co., 1897. Names many landlords.

HOAD, JOYCE. 'Using Chancery records', *O.F.H.* **3**(1), 1983, 9-13. Includes summaries of many Oxfordshire Chancery documents.

HOAD, JOYCE. 'Discoveries in Chancery', *O.F.H.* **3**(3), 1983, 85-7 & **3**(5), 1984, 166-8. Notes from Chancery records.

HOAD, JOYCE. 'Two Chancery cases', *O.F.H.* **3**(6), 1984, 211-12.

GIBSON, JEREMY. 'This stinking smoke', *C.&Ch.* **10**(5), 1987, 128-30. Lists persons examined by Exchequer commission, 1639, in a case concerning the sale of tobacco in Banbury.

WALTON, H.M. 'Quarter Sessions records in Oxfordshire and their uses for the genealogist', *O.F.H.* **2**(4), 1981, 99-103.

GRETTON, MARY STURGE, ed. *Oxfordshire justices of the peace in the seventeenth century.* O.R.S. **16**, 1934. Includes a calendar of the quarter sessions records, 1687-9.

BANNARD, H.E. 'The Berkshire, Buckinghamshire and Oxfordshire committees of 1642-1646', *B.B.O.A.J.* **31**, 1927, 173-92. Includes biographical notes on Parliamentary committeemen.

CHARITY COMMISSIONERS. *Reports of the Commissioners ... Oxford.* [ ], [1840?]. Reprinted volume including reports for the county 1815-39.

CHARITY COMMISSIONERS. *An abstract of the report of the Commissioners for inquiring concerning the charities of the City of Oxford, and the parishes of St.Giles, St.Clement, and Binsey.* Oxford: Munday & Slatter, 1823.

CHARITY COMMISSIONERS. *Reports of the Commissioners for inquiring concerning Charities in the Hundreds of Banbury and Bloxham, also some places in the Hundreds of Wootton, Ploughley, Chadlington and Bullingdon, Oxon., and a few places in Northamptonshire from the twelfth and thirteenth reports.* Banbury: J.G. Rusher, 1826.

B. *PAROCHIAL AND BOROUGH ADMINISTRATION*

The records of parochial government—the accounts of overseers, churchwardens and other parish officers, settlement papers, rate lists, etc.—contain much information of genealogical value. They frequently give the names, if nothing else, of the humble mass of the poor, who otherwise went unrecorded. Oxfordshire parochial records have been the subject of many books and articles. Some of those likely to be of genealogical interest are listed here. Some general works on the poor law are:

OLDHAM, C.R. 'Oxfordshire poor law papers', *Economic history review* **4**, 1932-4, 470-74, & **5**, 1934-5, 87-97. Includes list of poor law records amongst the archives of Quarter Sessions, and of relevant records from the Bampton parish chest.

BENTON, TONY. 'Sponsored migration under the new poor law', *O.F.H.* **2**(9), 1982, 286-8. Includes list of Oxfordshire migrants to northern textile towns.

HORN, PAMELA, ed. *Oxfordshire village life: the diaries of George James Dew (1846-1928), relieving officer.* Abingdon: Beacon Pubs., 1983. Gives many names.

The parochial records of Islington, Middlesex, contain many settlement examinations of Oxfordshire interest. See:

KELVIN, PATRICIA. 'Islington settlement examinations', *O.F.H.* **4**(7), 1988, 214-6.

Bampton

BLAIR, JOHN. 'Parish versus village: the Bampton Standlake tithe conflict of 1317-19', *O.L.H.* **2**(2), 1985, 34-47. Includes lists of householders of Hardwick and Brighthampton, 1279 and 1318.

Banbury

The following works are arranged chronologically:

Borough of Banbury, 1554-1954: Souvenir of Quarter-centenary of the granting of the Charter of Incorporation to the Borough of Banbury by Queen Mary on January 26th, 1554. Includes list of bailiffs and mayors, 1572-1954.

GIBSON, J.S.W., AND BRINKWORTH, E.R.C., eds. *Banbury Corporation records: Tudor and Stuart.* B.H.S. **15**, 1977. Includes several lists of inhabitants, with biographical notes on over 500 corporation members and officials, 1553-1732, and 13 pedigrees.

'Documents from St.Mary's church, Banbury', *C.&Ch.* **2**, 1962-5, 154-6. See also 7(4), 1977, 124. Lists documents found in the vestry and the vicarage.

POTTS, JOHN. *The bailiffs and mayors of the borough of Banbury, 1554 to 1904.* Banbury: [ ], 1904. List.

GILKES, R.K. 'Banbury: the pattern of local government 1554-1835', *C.&Ch.* **5**, 1971-4, 3-18 & 83-95. General discussion, including references to many potentially useful sources.

GILKES, R.W. 'The chamberlain and his role in local government in Banbury, 1554-1835', *C.&Ch.* **10**(2), 1986, 41-6 & **10**(3), 1986, 54-67. Lists chamberlains, etc.

GILKES, R.K. 'The town clerks of Banbury, 1554-1835', *C.&Ch.* **10**(7), 1987, 170-81. Identifies them.

CROUCH, COLIN. 'Banbury charities', *C.&Ch.* **11**(1), 1988, 2-15. Includes lists of officers, 17-20th c.

GIBSON, J.S.W. 'Trouble over sheep pens', *C.&Ch.* **7**(2), 1977, 35-48. Includes extensive list of persons concerned in a Banbury Exchequer case, 1656.

THWAITES, W. 'Banbury horse fairs in the 18th century', *C.&Ch.* **10**(5), 1987, 120-25. Discussion of the 'Toll Book for the Sale of Horses, 1753-1826', the latter lists buyers and sellers, with occupations and residences (not a transcript).

'Banbury parish ratebook, 1782', *C.&Ch.* **7**(7), 1978, 224-7. Full transcript of rate.

'Notes on the leaflet requesting the mayor of Banbury to call a public meeting, December 1792', *C.&Ch.* **7**(2), 1977, 51-4. Includes brief biographical notes on many prominent Banbury men.

Parochial and Borough Records *continued*

Banbury *continued*

RENOLD, P., ed. *Banbury gaol records*. B.H.S. 21, 1987. Gives many names of prisoners, and of police, lawyers, court officials, witnesses, etc., mainly 19th c. See also: PAIN, A.W. 'Banbury gaol records, 1829-1838', *C.&Ch.* 2, 1962-5, 194-5.

HORN, P. 'The Banbury workhouse child during the 1890s', *C.&Ch.* 5, 1971-4, 103-8 & 117-20. General discussion mentioning some names. See also Dorchester

Bicester

DUNKIN, JOHN. *The history and antiquities of Bicester* ... J. & A. Arch, 1816. Includes rental, 1325, priory accounts, 1425, monumental inscriptions, etc.

Bodicote

FEARON, J.H., ed. *Parish accounts for the 'town' of Bodicote, Oxfordshire, 1700-1822*. B.H.S. 12, 1975. Also includes land tax assessment, 1705, and lists of churchwardens, etc.
'Some notes on Bodicote', *C.&Ch.* 3, 1965-8, 131-4. Includes list of landowners, 1833, notes on 16 families, names from the hearth tax, 1665, extracts from churchwardens' accounts, etc.

Brighthampton

See Bampton

Burford

GRETTON, R.H. *The Burford records: a study in minor town government*. Oxford: Clarendon Press, 1920. Includes a 400 page calendar of the records.

Caversham

TOWNSEND, JOHN. *Caversham parish records*. Wokingham: the author, 1990. Includes 1821 census, settlement papers, removal orders, examinations, bastardy bonds, apprenticeship indentures, etc.

Dorchester

PEYTON, SIDNEY, A., ed. *The churchwardens' presentments in the Oxfordshire peculiars of Dorchester, Thame and Banbury*. O.R.S. 10, 1928. 17-19th c.

Eynsham

GIBSON, JEREMY. 'The fearfull fier at Ensham, whit Monday, 1629', *Eynsham record* 3, 1986, 14-16. See also 17-18. Includes list of those who lost their houses.

Eynsham *continued*

RICHARDS, DONALD. 'An Eynsham fire in 1696', *Eynsham record* 3, 1986, 19-21. Gives names of some sufferers, and other Eynsham inhabitants, from quarter sessions records.

Hardwick

See Bampton

Headington Union

MASON, EDNA. 'Headington Union', *O.F.H.* 5(3), 1989, 95-8. Describes poor law records.

Henley

BRIERS, P.M., ed. *Henley borough records: assembly books i-iv, 1395-1543*. O.R.S. 41, 1960.

Marston

WEAVER, F.W., AND CLARK, G.N., eds. *Churchwardens' accounts of Marston, Spelsbury, Pyrton*. O.R.S. 6, 1925. 16-17th c.

Oxford

The following works are listed in rough chronological order, beginning with general works:

GRAHAM, MALCOLM. 'Oxford city archives', *O.F.H.* 2(8), 1982, 245-9. Lists records.

MADAN, F. *Oxford city records*. [Oxford]: [the Corporation], 1887. Calendar of documents.

TURNER, W.H. 'On the municipal records of the City of Oxford', *O.A.H.S.P.* N.S. 3, 1880, 357-9. General discussion.

Oxford City records: catalogue of charters &c., 1199-1796, in the Town Clerk's strong room, Municipal Buildings, with the new pressmarks. Oxford: [the Corporation], 1899.

'[Brief notes on Oxford municipal archives]', *O.A.H.S.P.* N.S. 5, 1891, 347-9.

SALTER, H.E., ed. *Munimenta civitatis Oxonie*. O.H.S. 71, 1920. Medieval.

POLLARD, GRAHAM. 'The medieval town clerks of Oxford', *Ox.* 31, 1966, 43-76. Includes detailed biographical notes.

CAM, HELEN M. 'The hundred outside the North Gate of Oxford', *Ox.* 1, 1936, 113-28. Includes list of medieval bailiffs.

TURNER, WILLIAM H., ed. *Selections from the records of the City of Oxford, ... illustrating the municipal history ... 1509-1583*. Oxford: James Parker, 1880.

GREEN, JOHN RICHARD, AND ROBERSON, GEO. *Studies in Oxford history chiefly in the eighteenth century*. ed. C.L. Stainer. O.H.S. 41, 1909. Includes lists of civic officials, 1695-1835.

Oxford continued

SALTER, H.E., ed. 'Survey of Oxford in 1772', *O.H.S.* **75**, 1923, 1-82. Originally published O.U.P., 1912. Survey made under the Mileways Act, 1771, giving addresses and names of occupiers, with a measurement of their frontage.

St.Michaels

SALTER, H.E., ed. 'The churchwardens' accounts of St.Michael's church, Oxford', *O.A.S.* **78**, 1933, 1-292. 15-16th c.

St. Peter in the East

TYSSEN, A.D. 'On the old churchwardens' account books of St.Peter's-in-the-East', *O.A.H.S.P.* N.S. **1**, 1863, 286-302. Brief extracts, 17th c.

MYLNE, R.S. '[Churchwardens' accounts of St.Peter in the East, Oxford, 1444]', *Proceedings of the Society of Antiquaries of London* 2nd series **10**, 1883-5, 24-8.

Pyrton

See also Marston

Shipton under Wychwood

HOWARD-DRAKE, JOAN. 'The poor of Shipton under Wychwood parish, 1740-62', *Wychwoods history* **5**, 1989, 4-44. Includes many extracts from overseers' accounts, with lists of overseers and churchwardens.

South Newington

BRINKWORTH, E.R.C., ed. *South Newington churchwardens' accounts, 1553-1684.* B.H.S. **6**, 1964.

Spelsbury

OLDFIELD, J. 'A churchwarden's account book', *B.B.O.A.J.* **16**(1), 1910, 8-16. From Spelsbury. Brief extracts, 16-18th c.
See also Marston

Standlake

See Bampton

Tadmarton

MASON, JUDITH. 'The parish government of Tadmarton in the 18th and 19th centuries', *C.&Ch.* **2**, 1964, 127-30. Brief discussion.

Thame

ELLIS, W. PATTERSON, ed. 'The churchwardens' accounts of the parish of St.Mary, Thame', *B.B.O.A.J.* **7-20**, 1902-14, passim. 15th c.

LUPTON, H., ed. *Extracts from the accounts of the proctors and stewards of the Prebendal Church of the Blessed Virgin of Thame, commencing in the year 1529 and ending in the year 1641, and of the churchwardens of Thame, beginning in the year 1542.* Thame: H. Bradford, 1852.

PAYNE, E.J. 'The building of the Trinity aisle or north transept of Thame church, Oxfordshire, A.D. 1442', *O.A.H.S.P.* N.S. **1**, 1863, 268-83. Includes accounts giving names of tradesmen, etc.
See also Dorchester

Wigginton

PRICE, F.D., ed. *The Wigginton constable's book, 1691-1836.* B.H.S. **11**, 1971.

PRICE, F.D. 'A North Oxfordshire parish and its poor: Wigginton 1730-1830', *C.&Ch.* **2**, 1962-5, 1-6. General discussion.

Witney

BOLTON, JAMES L., AND MASLEN, MARJORIE M., eds. *Calendar of the court books of the Borough of Witney 1538-1610.* O.R.S. **54**. Includes list of bailiffs.

15. EDUCATIONAL RECORDS

The records of schools can provide the
genealogist with much information on teachers,
pupils, and others associated with them. Two
useful works on teachers in Oxfordshire are:

HORN, P. 'Oxfordshire village school teachers,
1800-1880', *C.&Ch.* **7**, 1976-9, 3-18. General
discussion, with some names.

HORN, PAMELA. 'Country teachers in Victorian
Oxfordshire: some case studies', *C.&Ch.* **10**(8),
1988, 202-13. Includes biographical notes.

A number of histories of individual schools have
been published, as have a few school registers,
and one log book. Log books are of particular
value to genealogists, but very few are in print.
That for Whitchurch listed below also has a wider
Oxfordshire interest, since it includes a
comprehensive listing of Oxfordshire school log
books. School histories usually list head teachers;
they may also give the names of other staff,
pupils, and others connected with the school.
Some, of course, are much more useful to the
genealogist than others. The following list is not
comprehensive, rather it aims to identify those
histories which may be of genealogical value.

Bicester

'The vicars school at Bicester in the 17th century',
O.A.S. **52**, 1907, 23-33. Includes names of
benefactors.

Bloxham

GIBSON, J.S.W. 'All Saints Grammar School,
Bloxham, 1853-1857', *C.&Ch.* **2**(6), 1963,
91-7. Includes list of boys 1853-6, and names of
local creditors.

SMITH, BRIAN S. *A history of Bloxham school.*
Bloxham: Bloxham School and the Old
Bloxhamist Society, 1978. Includes a useful list
of primary sources and gives many names.

*History of All Saints School, Bloxham, 1860-
1910.* Bloxham: the School, 1910. 2nd ed. 1925.
Includes list of masters and chaplains.

Burford

SIMPSON, A.M., AND RYLANDS, E. MOORE. *Burford
Grammar School, 1571-1971.* Burford: the
School, 1971. Includes list of headmasters.

Culham College

Culham College directory (1853-1951). Culham:
the College, 1951. Supplementary ed. 1955.
Lists students of a teacher training college.

Dorchester on Thames

Dorchester-on-Thames Grammar School.
Dorchester: Dorchester on Thames
Archaeology & Local History Group, [1976].
Lists 300 17-18th c. scholars.

Kingston Bagpuize

MUIR, JILL. 'Putting meat on the bones: a school
log book', *O.F.H.* **4**(4), 111-12. Entries relating
to the Ballard family of Kingston Bagpuize,
1902-4.

Oxford

*Christ Church Cathedral School: register of
choristers, probationers, masters, precentors,
organists from 1837-1900.* Salisbury: H.T.
Lancaster, 1900.

BOWEN, E.A., ed. *The register of the City of Oxford
High School, 1881-1925.* Oxford: privately
printed, 1938.

A Dragon roll. Oxford: Dragon School, 1969.

*Memorials of old boys and masters of the Dragon
School, Oxford who fell in the Great War.*
Oxford: O.U.P. for the School, 1922.
Biographies with portraits.

*Memorials of the old boys of the Dragon School,
Oxford, who gave their lives in the war of 1939-
1945.* Oxford: Basil Blackwell, 1948. Brief
biographies.

HARE, PATRICK. *Victorian masters: a biographical
essay on the nineteenth-century headmasters of
Magdalen College School, Oxford.* Oxford: [the
School], [1979].

STANIER, R.S. *Magdalen School: a history of
Magdalen College School, Oxford.* 2nd ed.
Oxford: Basil Blackwell, 1958. 1st edition also
published as *O.H.S.* N.S. **3**, 1940. Includes list
of masters and ushers, etc.

SPACKMAN, M. *History of the Oxford Central girl's
school and Cheney girl's grammar school.*
Abingdon: Abbey Press, 1974. Includes
reminiscences of many former students.

HILL, R.D. *A history of St.Edwards School, 1863-
1963.* 7th ed. Altrincham: John Sherratt & Son,
1962. Oxford school; includes some names.

The roll of St.Edward's School, 1863-1939. 5th
ed. Oxford: Oxonian Press, 1939.

Thame

BROWN, J. HOWARD. *A short history of Thame
school, of the foundation of Sir John Williams,
Knight, Lord Williams of Thame.* Hazell,
Watson & Viney, 1927. Includes notes on
headmasters, etc.

Whitchurch

HORN, PAMELA, ed. *Village education in
nineteenth-century Oxfordshire: the
Whitchurch school log book, 1868-93 and other
documents*. O.R.S. **51**, 1979. Many names,
includes a list of Oxfordshire school log books.

Williamscote

LOVEDAY, THOMAS, ed. 'The registers of
Williamscote School', *C.&Ch.* **2**, 1963, 39-48.
1575-1656.
'The charity boys of Williamscote school in 1820
and 1821', *C.&Ch.* **2** 1962-5, 98-9. List of boys.

Witney

FLEMING, MARY A. *Witney Grammar School, 1660-
1960*. Oxford: O.U.P., 1960. Includes a useful
list of primary sources.

16. EMIGRATION

Many Oxfordshire people have migrated to
distant climes. In order to trace them, it is
frequently necessary to undertake research in both
England and the country they settled in. It is not
the intention here to list everything published on
Oxfordshire emigrants, but rather to indicate a
few readily available works which may be useful.
Further assistance may be had by consulting the
works listed in chapter 17 of *English genealogy:
an introductory bibliography.*

Australia

GIBSON, J.S.W. 'Sponsored emigration of paupers
from Banbury Union, 1834-1860', *O.F.H.* **2**(7),
1982, 211-15. Includes list, 1836-59, of
emigrants to Canada and Australia.

MCKAY, BARRY. *Tackley to Tasmania: pauper
emigration from an Oxfordshire village to
Australia and the wreck of the Cataraqui, 1845.*
Tackley: Tackley Local History Group, 1980.
Includes list of Oxfordshire emigrants lost.

WALKER-SMITH, J.A. 'A convict ancestor', *O.F.H.*
2(3), 1980, 70-71. How the Buckingham family
tree was traced through Australian convict
records.

Canada

See Australia

New Zealand

ARNOLD, ROLLO. *The farthest promised land:
English villagers, New Zealand immigrants of
the 1870s.* Wellington: Victoria University
Press, 1981. Includes many names of
Oxfordshire migrants from the Wychwood area,
who are listed in: GIBSON, J.S.W. 'Early 1870s
emigrants to New Zealand', *O.F.H.* **3**(2), 1983,
67-9.

DEELEY, WILMA. 'Emigrants from Oxfordshire to
Canterbury, New Zealand', *O.F.H.* **5**(6), 1990,
243-5. Brief list, late 19th c.

South Africa

WILLIAMS, J. ROBERT. 'Oxfordshire settlers in the
Eastern Cape, 1820', *O.F.H.* **2**(9), 1982, 293-4.
Includes list.

United States

'Early colonists', *O.F.H.* **1**(5), 1978, 132. Brief
list of Oxfordshire migrants to New England,
1620-50.

TRINDER, BARRIE. 'The distant scene: Banbury and
the United States in the mid-nineteenth
century', *C.&Ch.* **7**(6), 1978, 163-74. Includes
brief discussion of emigration.

FAMILY NAME INDEX

PLACE NAME INDEX

AUTHOR INDEX